THE END OF HUMANISM

Library of Congress Cataloging in Publication Data
The End of Humanism: Writings on Performance
Library of Congress Catalog Card No.: 82-62094
ISBN: 0-933826-18-4
ISBN: 0-933826-19-2 (paper)

Design: Gautam Dasgupta

Printed in the United States of America

Publication of this book has been made possible in part by grants from the
National Endowment for the Arts, Washington, D.C., a federal agency,
and public funds received from the New York State Council on the Arts.

The End of Humanism

Writings on Performance

RICHARD SCHECHNER

Performing Arts Journal Publications
New York

This is the second volume of the Performance Studies Series edited by Brooks McNamara and Richard Schechner. The first volume was Victor Turner's *From Ritual to Theatre: The Human Seriousness of Play*.

GENERAL INTRODUCTION TO THE PERFORMANCE STUDIES SERIES

What is a performance? A play? Dancers dancing? A concert? What you see on TV? Circus and Carnival? A press conference by whoever is President? The shooting of the Pope as portrayed by media—or the instant replays of Lee Harvey Oswald being shot? And do these events have anything to do with ritual, a week with Grotowski in the woods outside of Wroclaw, or a Topeng masked dance drama as performed in Peliatan, Bali? Performance is no longer easy to define or locate: the soncept and structure has spread all over the place. It is ethnic and intercultural, historical and ahistorical, aesthetic and ritual, sociological and political. Performance is a mode of behavior, an approach to experience; it is play, sport, aesthetics, popular entertainments, experimental theatre, and more. But in order for this broad perspective to develop, performance must be written about with precision and in full detail. The editors of this Series have designed it as a forum for investigating what performance is, how it works, and what its place in postmodern society may be. Performance Studies is not properly theatrical, cinematic, anthropological, historical, or artistic—though any of the monographs in the Series incorporate one or more of these disciplines. Because we are fostering a new approach to the study of performance, we have kept the Series open-ended in order to incorporate new work. The Series, we hope, will measure the depth and breadth of the field—and its fertility: from circus to Mabou Mines, rodeo to healing rites, Black performance in South Africa to the Union City Passion Play. Performance Studies will be available for scholars in all areas of performance as well as for theatre workers who want to expand and deepen their notions of performance.

Brooks McNamara
Richard Schechner

To
Joel and Eve Schwarz

from striped bass to chess on the road to knowing

Contents

Acknowledgements

All the writings in this book originally appeared in journals—and I thank the editors of these publications not only for printing my work but for permitting me to collect them now in this volume. "Decline and Fall of the (American) Avant-Garde, extensively revised for this book, came out first in *Performing Arts Journal.* So did "The End of Humanism." An earlier version of "The End of Humanism" was published by the *Soho Weekly News.* "The Natural/Artificial Controversy Renewed" appeared in *The Bennington Review;* "The Crash of Performative Circumstances" was published by *Tri-Quarterly.*

Thank You

Carol Martin edited and helped revise "Decline & Fall of the (American) Avant-Garde." Edie and Victor Turner have engaged me in an ongoing dialogue regarding both performance aesthetic and ritual. My colleagues in the Department of Performance Studies, Tisch School of the Arts, NYU, have helped me develop ideas that I often feel pass through me but are not mine. The many people I've worked with in the theatre—from members of The Performance Group to people in various workshops and productions beyond TPG—have had the deepest impact on my thinking. I remember a Talmudic saying that was a favorite of my grandfather Samuel Schwarz who was my first teacher: "Much have I learned from my teachers, even more from my friends, but from my students most of all." True.

Preface

Why the "end of humanism"? I think of myself as a humanist. As a person who wants to see preserved the "human values" of compassion, individual expression, various and sundry freedoms (expression, opportunity, religion, etc.: those proclaimed by the American Declaration of Independence and Constitution; good 18th century rationalist values). Yet humanism as an ideology is also very connected to the sense that human beings, male human beings especially ("man" to use another 18th century term), are the lords and masters of the world. And not just this planet earth, but the whole creation. "Man is the measure of all things," someone of the Italian Renaissance said. Da Vinci made his famous drawing of a male with his arms outstretched, not in crucifixion but in measurement. A noble idea, actually, this one that human values are the only values. But also an idea that has led to extreme cruelty. How? George Orwell put it briefly thus: All animals are equal but some are more equal than others. So if "man is the measure," which of the several billion men are entitled to set the standards of measurement?

And what of non-human beings? Animals, plants; maybe even the planet itself (or is it "herself"?). And the cosmos . . . who is measuring the cosmos? Not the soccer team but the whole creation. I think the humanist idea is a bit early. It needs revision to include all people; and then it needs to be married to certain values that we, as a species, not only enunciate but internalize. The "rights of people" must be as "natural" to our species as having ten fingers. Until that time human beings aren't ready for humanism.

So what do I propose to take humanism's place?

Respect for the planet and all what dwells therein. Measure humans against planetary needs, not the other way around. And see the planet against the field of the cosmos. No one really knows what the needs of the cosmos might be, if any.

This book isn't directly about such grand issues. It's a more limited book. But each of the writings in this book signals a turning away from classical humanism toward some kind of planetary interculturalism. I don't claim that these writings hang together to make some fully integrated whole. My clearest theme is an analytic one: What is experimental theatre in America; what happened to it; and what's happening now after a period of intense activity has subsided? I feel we as a culture, as a set of cultures, are passing into our "postmodern" phase. And I feel that I as an individual have entered a period of reflection: where my writing as a function of my thinking takes over from my theatre directing which is a function of my doing.

In this meditative mood I address my colleagues in and out of theatre. I wish this book to be part of a dialogue.

New York
July, 1982

THE DECLINE AND FALL
OF THE (AMERICAN)
AVANT-GARDE

The Decline and Fall
of the (American)
Avant-Garde

A Note From June 1982

An essay like this is never finished. It always brings with it a sense of its own unspoken alternatives. It would be neater to say "development," as if I could foresee the future. But I can't. At best I can report on what I think are trends or tendencies. These are curves of experience measured against my own theories: my sense of how these curves will work themselves out in the future.

And about the future—not only of theatre, but of the world (if you permit me that *hubris*)—I am of a mixed opinion. There is close to me my own belly, my own intimate sense of how it's all going to turn out. Well, I have a son and want more children; I buy books; I make plans to direct plays; I write furiously and lovingly. So the evidence suggests that I expect a future, a future that is okay. Not only for me but for those close to me: family, friends, colleagues—people I respect and interact with. But there is another sense of future, one guided not by the belly-feel but by what my analytic intellect constructs from what's going on all around the world. This future proclaims danger, even terror and doom. On several levels, from the most intense, almost unimaginable globacide brought on by nuclear war to ecological catastrophe brought on by the mess technological-industrial operations have made of the environment. And there are the "simple" miseries that have long been the companion of the human condition: hunger, poverty, ignorance, exploitation, tyranny: the failure of humankind to put our own houses in order. We have the ideals, maybe even the ideologies, to do better. Every system broadcasts its desire to guarantee the greatest good for the greatest number—and then acts to enhance the power of its own oligarchy. Thus between published utopias and the daily experience of billions of human beings comes unspeakable misery.

Now my corner of experience, my "specialty," is performance. Not just theatre, but performance as a wide variety of activities ranging from theatre and dance to sports, rituals, popular entertainments, therapies that use performance techniques, and ordinary daily encounters among people where participants seem to be playing out roles more than just "being themselves." I've even come to doubt that there is a core or single self that a person can "be." Everything in human behavior indicates that we perform our existence, especially our social existence. In this writing I am talking about a corner of my corner: the American experimental theatre from about the mid-1950s to the present. The essay that is the basis of this longer, more thought-out writing appeared in two successive issues of *Performing Arts Journal* in 1981 (numbers 14 and 15). And then in PAJ 16 some replies to my article appeared. Replies, or alternative opinions about the avant-garde, also appeared with some regularity in the *Village Voice* and the now defunct *Soho Weekly News* during the fall and winter of 1981-82.

I knew my writing touched a nerve, and hurt. For I was saying that something full, innovative, and promising was over. But I was also saying more than that: something different and possibly new was forthcoming. I'm writing these sentences in Manhattan on 11 June 1982. Tomorrow a great rally and march will gather near the United Nations and move to Central Park. Five hundred thousand people, maybe more, will demonstrate against nuclear arms. A definite nostalgia for the '60s is being evoked. The Bread and Puppet Theatre has distributed leaflets asking for "250 people and musicians to participate in the End of the World Pageant" and "800 people needed for Giant Puppet Parade!" It may be that we are entering a new period of social activism; that the decline in experimental performance that I describe in this essay is ending. Perhaps connections will be made between the resources spent on armaments and the resources withheld from meeting human needs. This funneling of energy from human needs to death is not an American sin only; it affects almost every nation, all societies. To oppose the war industries means, finally, to develop a strong political viewpoint. If the disarmament movement becomes powerful politically, as it has the chance to be, its politics cannot be identical to the politics of the '60s. To make way for new politics—and for new arts, new experiments in the theatre—nostalgia must be gotten rid of. I welcome the Bread and Puppet. At the same time, and even more eagerly, I await meeting tomorrow new groups with new methods.

Some critics of my PAJ essay said I was speaking only for myself—that I erred in expanding my experiences into general principles, that I was "mythologizing." It's true that I speak from the point of view of what happened to me. I also talk about work that I have seen of others. I use my experience as doer and observer as the basis for generalizations about experimental performance in America. Why not? I am opposed to the division between doers, critics, and theorists; and I prefer to work from primary sources: what I've done, what I've seen. Working this way does not reduce my arguments to personalism. On the contrary, reasoning from experience gives my position material solidity.

I expect people to disagree. I welcome debate.

Two Kinds of Avant-Garde

The term "avant-garde" is a label for two very different kinds of activity. First there is the "historical avant-garde" comprised of very definite movements, some of them originating almost 100 years ago. The historical avant-garde consists of movements that were, some of which continue, like surrealism, and some of which have passed away, like futurism. The second kind of avant-garde is what I call "experimental" performance: whatever is happening at the boundaries, in advance of the mainstream. Of course, sometimes these two kinds of avant-gardes are expressed in the same movement. Still, it is necessary to distinguish between them. To do so more clearly I shall say a few things further about each.

1. The historical avant-garde is known by its many examples: symbolism, futurism, expressionism, constructivism, surrealism, dada; and since World War II, in theatre, as poor theatre, environmental theatre, guerrilla theatre, alternative theatre, theatre of images—and dozens of other movements. Does this proliferation signal an ever-deepening alienation from society of artists and a concomitant disintegration of values, or does it mark the appearance of a fundamental new value: pluralism, what has been known also as the postmodern?

The historical avant-garde can be seen as wave after wave of anti-bourgeois, mostly left-leaning, angry yet visionary artists pouring themselves out onto a hostile shore (a beach-head, to use the obvious military metaphor). Each wave is soaked up by the society it apparently hates and opposes—co-opted and made fashionable, turned into style. Soho, the neighborhood south of Houston Street in Manhattan that began as an outpost of experimental art and performance, has become a precinct of chi-chi dress shops and restaurants symbiotically connected to equally fashionable galleries and performing spaces.

But each wave, at the outset, when it is fresh and full of energy, proclaims its program, its manifesto, for changing the world. This single-mindedness of each avant-garde seems laughable when measured against the great number of avant-gardes this century has witnessed; and steadily it becomes clearer that the new abiding quality is pluralism. Pluralism undercuts any specific utopian or apocalyptic vision. As an historian of the avant-garde, Matei Calinescu has said:

The avant-garde has consistently seen its major task of "changing life" (Rimbaud) as achievable primarily through a revolution of artistic form. [. . .] The possibility of the avant-garde is linked to the existence of a clearly identifiable enemy (and "official culture," a dogmatically imposed system of values) and when such an enemy fails to materialize, or, worse, becomes hard even to imagine, the avant-garde loses, together with its polemical *raison d'être*, its main asset, its youthful vitality. [. . .] The great challenge that the "ideology" of the avant-garde has had to face all through the twentieth century but most particularly in the post-World War II period, has been without doubt the rise in the West of cultural pluralism.[1]

In other essays in this book I explore this pluralism, along with other aspects of the postmodern. Here I want to point out that in today's world, according to Calinescu, and I agree, there is no reason for still another wave of the historical avant-garde to exist. There is no single enemy. Artists are as likely to be part of as apart from the Establishment—if one counts as the Establishment the public monies of the various state and federal endowments. Theatre experiments take place even at the Metropolitan Opera House when Robert Wilson mounts a production there. Or look at the fruitful relationship between Joseph Papp's Public Theatre and Mabou Mines and Richard Foreman. Not to mention the sponsorship of all kinds of experimental works by the Shah of Iran at Shiraz. Nor can the avant-garde be identified as a movement or a system of movements. At best the term "avant-garde" is vague, meaning anything from experimental work to working with very little money; from stylish performances not yet seen on Broadway to a small band of artists whose reputation is such that they can raise immense amounts of money to sponsor new works. There is no unity, no sense of shared purpose. The historical avant-garde has been stalemated.

The remnants and inheritors of the historical avant-garde no longer imagine themselves as belonging to a single movement at all. Certainly no artist I know, or have heard of, seriously thinks that through art the order of society will change. Rather artists see themselves as so many alternatives—trees with many branches, forests of branching trees. As such each avant-garde, each group, almost each individual artist, is just one more style among many. These styles compete for attention, for dominance. You are as likely to find them in *Vogue* or the gossip columns of *People* as anywhere else.

What's happened over a century's time, chastened by what's happened in the world during that period, is that artists have ceased believing in the efficacy of art while still mouthing the slogans, and going through the motions, of making art to change the world. And the ideologies and techniques of earlier avant-gardes, often preserved as never before on film and sound recordings, are lying around conveniently ready to be picked through, re-cycled, and called to active duty. What began before World War I as a bur-ning involvement of artists in the future of their societies—if only as outcasts who believed that someday they would be regarded as prophets (Artaud, Brecht)—subsided by the time of the mid-70s into an acknowledgement that artistic programs would not be, could never be, lived by the vast ma-jority of people. This loss of hope transformed each avant-garde, in turn, into an "artistic style." As the years passed an "historical sense" settled in on the avant-garde; a revision of the history of the avant-garde along the lines Calinescu outlines took place. Richard Foreman may still write mani-festoes—scholars file them in a drawer marked "M."

2. The second meaning of avant-garde is to be experimental. The roots of the word "experimental mean to "go beyond the boundaries"—ex/peri: To venture into the unknown; to try out new things; to test hypotheses against experience. Experience is of course a word whose roots are identical to experiment; the two concepts as actions are inextricably connected to each other.

Although artistic and scientific experimentation are somewhat alike there are big differences too. In science experiments must be testable; ideally at least every experiment is a prediction whose outcome adds to the ever-ex-panding store of established knowledge. Artistic experiments add to spheres of experience rather than knowledge. Furthermore, the realms of art are made from not only what is but from whatever can be imagined, proposed, invented. As Victor Turner puts it, artistic creativity functions in the sub-junctive mood; the artist "makes believe" in two senses: first, as that phrase is ordinarily understood; secondly, as artistic work creates the belief-world in which it exists.

Most experiments in performance since 1975 have been in terms of form. Performance artists were not so concerned with what they were saying as with the means of communicating, the places where the events took place, the persons employed as performers, the relationship to the audience. The Living Theatre, the Bread and Puppet Theatre, the San Francisco Mime Troupe, and the Teatro Campesino excepted, other major groups and art-ists followed the conceptual lead of people like John Cage, Jerzy Grotowski, and Peter Brook in seeking mainly to find new ways, new places, and new audience relationships for theatre. I am in no way denying or denegrating the importance of these formal experiments. I am saying that the time is ripe today to join new techniques with content. I see some of that, for ex-ample, in Mabou Mines'/JoAnne Akalaitis's *Dead End Kids*. But also I see much sterile repetition of old experiments.

Experiments in performance after the end of the Vietnam War were mostly formal because artists did not believe that their art could effect social change. At best, in punk rock, in some of the work of Wooster Group, there was, and is, a nihilistic cry of pain and rage. New technologies were used, but often intentionally distorted or destroyed as if these very technologies were more threatening than liberating. The historical avant-garde was dead. Experimental art, or non-art, claimed the only legitimacies. The intensive activity accompanying the protests against the Vietnam War actually lasted a very few years, from around 1964 to 1973, with most of the activity coming from 1967 on, cresting in 1970, and then subsiding. Once the War ended and the recession of the mid-'70s hit, artists fell into a formalist deep freeze. Great work was done, but it was cut off: it did not manifest significant content. Instead a certain kind of "high art obscurity" took over, seen clearly in the work of the period's leading artists: Robert Wilson, Richard Foreman, Mabou Mines, Merce Cunningham, Simone Forti, Grand Union. We are still waiting for the formalist experiments to be translated into content.

At present, witnessed by the Gathering of August 1981 in St. Peter, Minnesota, that brought together dozens of "grass roots" theatre groups, and the surge of people, many performing artists, participating in the Disarmament Movement, there is a growing popular—ought I to say "populist"?—movement that may spell the end of formalist isolation.[2] I don't want to downplay the Gathering, or the outpouring of people for the great anti-nuclear rally of 1982 in New York. Still it's too early to say what these movements signify theatrically speaking. So in this writing I will concentrate on the period of great experimental activity of the '60s and '70s, outlining what I believe are the causes of that activity's demise.

The Homeric Lists of the '60s and '70s

In the American theatre, what a burst of experimental energy there was from the '50s to around 1975. It was a rolling in of still another wave of the "historical avant-garde," but it was more, too. Not only directors, but authors, performers, composers, visual artists, designers, technicians, managers, worked in such a profusion of forms, spaces, social contexts, for so many different reasons: from "pure art" to anarchistic politics, from personal, even intimate, expression and revelation (always open to the charge "is what you're doing theatre or therapy?") to collective statements of archetypal imagery, from fierce assertions of what Ralph Ortiz called "paleologic," (what people of today might call "right brain dominance") to uses of theatre and dance as a means of exploring cognitive systems of thought. In rooms, in theatres, in the streets, in lettuce fields and cotton fields, in workplaces (factories, storefronts), in hospitals, prisons, and other "total institutions," in gathering-places (railroad stations, laundromats), in galleries, in schools—you name the place, theatre was there—live performance literally was everywhere trying to do everything. And working with so many different kinds of people: professional performers and artists, people from "the community," migrant farmers and laborers, poor people, prisoners, inmates, crazies, people of all races and ethnic groups, all economic classes and political convictions.

A theatre engaged. Engaged for and against. Committed to a network of struggles: political, social, aesthetic, environmental. Against the war in Vietnam and America's involvement in it on behalf of the corrupt South Vietnamese government; for racial equality and opportunity; against environmental degradation; for nuclear disarmament; against the military-industrial corporate multinational state (a mouthful); for women's rights, gay rights. A theatre that was genuinely intercultural, drawing its techniques and examples from within the Euro-American culture area, and from without—from Africa, Asia, Native America, Micronesia: everywhere.

People didn't question too much whether or not this interculturalism—this affection for Kathakali exercises, the precision of Noh drama, the simultaneity and intensity of African dance—was a continuation of colonialism, a further exploitation of other cultures. There was something simply celebratory about discovering how diverse the world was, how many performance genres there were, and how we could enrich our own experience by borrowing, stealing, exchanging. At that time the seeds of a few intercultural companies were sown: Brook's Centre in Paris, Terayama's brand of surrealism in Tokyo, Grotowski's move outside theatre. Each of these experiments owed much to the American experiences of their companies' members. In Denmark, Eugenio Barba began work that led to his experiments in "Theatre Anthropology."

Amidst this boiling activity deep questions of aesthetics were probed as they hadn't been before. What is a theatre? Where does it take place? Is that place "sacred" or special? Is there such a thing as "secular ritual"? Is that what theatre is? Who performs in a theatre? Why? Are these people different or special? Where is the center of theatrical activity? Does the text (still) have primacy? Should theatre artists "serve" the playwright by "interpreting" his text? And if the text is not the most important thing, what is? Should a theatrical event—no longer a play, a performance, a drama: but an "event"—proceed in a linear way, and if not, what gives it unity? Does it need unity? What is unity? It is differently understood by Aristotle, Brecht, Artaud, and the authors of the Sanskrit treatise on theatre, *Natyasastra*. What is the relationship between theatre, dance, popular entertainments, religious rituals, therapy, games, sports, children's play, the personae politicians and other public figures display? Can a "universal performance theory" be developed to explain all these "performative genres"? Is such a theory important to the practical work of making theatre? How should the audience get involved in the event, if at all: as watchers, doers, witnesses, total participants as in Grotowski's paratheatrical work since 1967? Should audiences mind their own business and just watch?

Often I was accused, in those days, of "forced participation," as if spectators could be coerced into joining such productions as *Dionysus in 69* or *Commune.* Was peer pressure and manipulation the equivalent of coercion? How should performers be trained? If the system of Stanislavski is no longer adequate, if it ever was, what can replace it? Are Asian forms of training—from Kathakali, yoga, t'ai chi, Noh, Kabuki, Chinese Opera—relevant; will such training help bring forth a different kind of American performer? And once performers are trained in what ways can they express themselves? Are they always to be servants of authors, directors, or designers? Must peformers always wear the masks of characters? Is the best they can hope for the temporary stepping aside suggested by Brecht (who then, himself, as playwright-director, controlled what the actor said about the character)? Many performers wanted to rip off this mask of character, a mask built by authors who literally put words in the mouths of actors; and then those words, and the actors' very bodies, were reformed by directors who in composing the *mises en scène* lay one more mask over the actor. First the author's and later the director's authority was challenged and overturned.

So many questions still unanswered.

For a few years—working sometimes in collaboration, sometimes in competition, sometimes in ignorance of each other—performers, directors, choreographers, composers (in more than the musical sense), authors, and designers each functioned as "primary creators." The traditional "triangle" of theatrical elements was turned over and over.

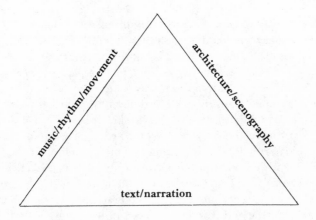

Traditionally, in Euro-American theatre, the "text/narration" is the base of the performance triangle; but in the experimental theatre of the '60s and '70s each side of the triangle was used as the basis for work. This meant that events of radically different kinds were generated. Sometimes the actor dominated, sometimes movement and dance, sometimes the visual, sometimes the sonic, sometimes the scenographic/architectural. Rarely, but radiantly, all elements came together in extraordinary harmony. This I experienced in Grotowski's *Akropolis,* the Living's *Mysteries,* the Open's *Serpent,* the Manhattan Project's *Alice,* Mabou Mines' *Red Horse,* Foreman's *Sophia = Wisdom: The Cliffs,* Wooster Group's *Rumstick Road,* and Kantor's *The Dead Class.*

There were so many unexpected, uninhibited exchanges among visual artists, actors, choreographers, musicians, dancers, social activists, scientists, directors, authors, ritualists, and ordinary people who got up from their seats (if there were any) and joined the performances that we believed we could together renew the world. In that hope we were yet another wave of the historical avant-garde. Riding that wave left little time for meditation on what would happen when it crashed on shore, reversed current, and became swept up in the inevitable backwash.

So though it had to happen it still came as a surprise when much, if not all, of this activity—the experiments, the breaking of boundaries and conventions, the political action, the questioning, the multiplicity of staging options, the sharing of primary creative authority—subsided. Many activities went forward—there is much more work going on today than in 1955—but the sense of movement, or general, collective action, went. A big bang was succeeded by entropy. It's my purpose here to investigate the entropy: to look it straight in its foggy face. And, frankly, to pick up seeds in the dust.

First, let no one be surprised that a creative period in the theatre flashes by in what feels like an instant. In Western theatre, at least, that's the tradition. From the first play of Aeschylus to the last plays of Euripides and Sophocles (who barely out-lived his younger colleague) is sixty-seven years (472-405 B.C.); from Marlowe's *Tamburlaine* to Middleton and Rowley's *The Changeling* a brief thirty-five years (1587-1622) containing all the great Elizabethan-Jacobean theatre. From the Cage-Cunningham performance at Black Mountain College to the closing of Richard Foreman's theatre on lower Broadway is twenty-seven years (1952-1979).

Think of the people who experimented during those twenty-seven years—whose work first came to the attention of each other and the public during that time. Think of Cage, Beck, Malina, Valdez, Schumann, Chaikin, Schechner, Breuer, van Itallie, Terry, Rainer, Halprin, Forte, Dunn, Weiss, Zank, Ludlam, Vaccaro, Carmines, Fornes, Gregory, Kaprow, LeCompte, Gray, Kirby, Davis, O'Neal, Moses, Bullins, Mcbeth, Davis, Glass, Monk, Forti, Paxton, Brown, Childs, Akalaitis, Wilson, Foreman

. . . and many more. Think also of those stalwarts of each group who form-ed the muscle, bone, and sinew of the movement—performers such as those in The Performance Group: MacIntosh, Borst, Gray, Shelton, Griffiths, Sack; designers Rojo and Clayburgh; technicians Rayvid and Porter; business people Smith, Ross, Locitzer. I name some from TPG because I worked with them. But each group had its core: its Ben Israels, Zimets, Maleczechs, Raymonds, Setterfields, Manheims. On and on. The names need to be on a plaque somewhere, these people who worked with all their lives' energies. Some, not named, authentic unknown soldiers of ex-perimental theatre, had their lives wrecked.

Maybe you know these people not by their individual names but their collective banners, for this was an age of groups, communes, collectives. The Living Theatre, Teatro Campesino, Bread and Puppet, Open Theater, Performance Group, Mabou Mines, Ontological-Hysteric Theater, Ridiculous Theatrical Company, Play-House of the Ridiculous, San Francisco Mime Troupe, San Francisco Dancers' Workshop, Judson Dance Theatre, Judson Poets' Theater, Caffe Cino, La Mama ETC, Theatre Genesis, OM Theatre Workshop, Firehouse Theatre, The Byrd Hoffman Foundation, Provisional Theatre, Grand Union, The Iowa Theatre Lab, The Manhattan Project, The House, Structuralist Work-shop, Free Southern Theatre, Pageant Players, New Lafayette Theatre, Spirit House.[3] Or maybe you know them by their ideological monikers: en-vironmental theatre, poor theatre, Happenings, black theatre, guerilla theatre, workers' theatre, peoples' theatre, postmodern performance, theatre of mixed means, intermedia . . . and more. There was no single ideology or umbrella heading. Or maybe you know them by the titles of some of their key productions, events, activities, creations, or composi-tions—for it was hard even to assign a definite genre to what was happen-ing. Think of *The Connection, Frankenstein, Paradise Now, The Serpent, Termin-al, Dionysus in 69, B-Beaver Animation, Shaggy Dog Animation, Bluebeard, Camille, When Queens Collide, Life and Times of Joseph Stalin, Einstein on the Beach, Vertical Mobility, Rhoda in Potatoland, Rumstick Road, Alice in Wonder-land, Domestic Resurrection Circus, Trio A, August Moon, Photoanalysis, Slaveship, Clara's Old Man, Riot, The Mother*; or performances of *Godot* before mostly poor blacks in Louisiana, Alabama, and Mississippi during "freedom sum-mer" 1964; or Happenings in parks, bus stations, abandoned airstrips, art galleries. Or theatre during the great demonstrations against the Vietnam War in 1967 and 1970, or the celebration-riot called Festival of Life put to-gether by Abbie Hoffman, Jerry Rubin, and several theatrical colleagues for the National Convention of the Democratic Party in Chicago in 1968. What's amazing about this Homer's List is that so many of these events were "significant": they added to our understanding of theatre, they were critiques of our society, they suggested new ways of performing. And taken together, they got to a lot of people.

Homer's list of ships, or one of those Abraham-begat-Isaac genealogies of the Bible. My intent is roughly the same: remember how many we were, how brave, how full of time and hope; how the world was to be reconstructed if not in our images then in the images we called into being by dint of our doings. Or the list sounds elegiac: how many have fallen.

The Living Theatre is living in Italy, while in America ex-Living actor Steve Ben Israel performs his bitter-sweet stand-up comic routine about the old days; the Campesino turned from standing with strikers to kneeling in front of the Virgin (still supporting the farmworkers, but more in tune with an old religious ideology whose ultimate value to the workers can be questioned); the Bread and Puppet, which once performed with regularity on the New York City streets, now visits here only occasionally, or for very special purposes such as the June '82 anti-Nuke demonstration; the Open disbanded in the early '70s only to have Chaikin band some alumni together for a series of projects none of which burned the mind; most of those I worked with in TPG have moved on, and the Group is now re-christened Wooster; Foreman's theatre is closed and his work in America is mostly directing other peoples' scripts. The Manhattan Project, Pageant Players, Judson Poets' and Judson Dancers' Theatres, Grand Union, New Lafayette, Caffe Cino, Theatre Genesis, Play-House of the Ridiculous—all are gone. Ellen Stewart at La Mama still sponsors experimental work, including very fine imports. Joseph Papp at the Public has given a home to Mabou Mines. But the heart of the movement is stopped.

Performance art and work that is in between music, dance, and theatre—like punk, new wave: whatever's in—flourishes, both in New York and around the country, on the West Coast especially. Happenings are done on commission for galleries and on campuses. All this is as it should be—but there should be more: the sideshows have become the main event. Something's screwy.

Although many of the people previously named still work in theatre, or some aspect of performance, and some groups still exist, the collective output of the people and groups no longer dominates consciousness. The scene isn't so important—it's not implicated or even consulted in rethinking society. Once more performance is ephemeral. I look at the period from the mid-'50s through the '70s and see the people, the groups, the works in receding perspective: a parade passed, with reverberations from ever more distant drums; or a thunderstorm come and gone, with an occasional flash still visible, but no promise of more.

The Expanded Field of Performance

What the experimental theatre accomplished was to expand radically the field of performance—to redefine what a performance was, where it could take place, who it involved, how it could be constructed, who or what could generate it. Even though we are today in a period of extreme formalism and nihilism the accomplishments of the experimentalists can later be put to work. The qualities of the expanded field of performance can be summarized by outlining all the ways performances can be generated. There are at least eight:

1. Plays. No need to further discuss what is meant by this.

2. Theories. The ideas of people like Cage, Kaprow, Kirby, Grotowski, Foreman, Schechner not only explained their own work, and what they thought theatre could be, but directly instigated the creation of new kinds of performances, new combinations.

3. Group-created works. Productions such as *The Rhode Island Trilogy*, the *Animations* series, *Alice in Wonderland, Mutation Show, Frankenstein*, the Bread and Puppet pageants, and so on were not the work of a single author but of collectives. Hundreds of such works were made during the period.

4. Performer-created works. People like Spalding Gray, Leeny Sack, Bob Carroll, Jeff Weiss, Steve Ben Israel, Stuart Sherman make their own performances.

5. Performance art. Happenings, "California art," visual artists doing performances—people who work outside of their expected contexts.

6. Political theatre. Street theatre, guerrilla theatre, protest marches and demonstrations, "Invisible" and "Forum" theatre.[3]

7. Workshops and paratheatre. Grotowski's experiments since 1967; Barba's "Theatre Anthropology,"[4] Iowa Theatre Lab's August Moon, the Gathering, Anna Halprin's "rituals" created with the San Francisco Dancer's Workshop, and so important to people who made the Judson Dance Theatre. Any number of "human potential" or "growth" activities and workshops that are in between theatre and therapy and religion.

8. Relgious ceremonies as theatre. The Dervishes on tour, Yoshi Oida's performances, the growing number of anthropologists who regard religious ceremonies as performance.

What happened during the '60s and into the '70s was that performances originated from many centers other than dramatic texts. Theories about what performance was, or could be, gave rise to events rarely if ever seen before. Groups as such were used as collective authors—instead of getting people together to "do a play" people who were working together "looked for material" from which to "make a performance." Even individual performers developed their own shows, importing into the avant-garde techniques that earlier belonged mostly to popular culture. Visual artists came down off the wall, first creating environments and then events to take place within these environments. From the marriage between pop culture and visual arts arose Happenings and performance art. Dancers started to speak and use both narrative and non-linear verbal and visual material. The long and close association of Cage and Cunningham helped greatly in bringing together dancers, musicians, and visual artists whose particular skills were "rubbed against each other" rather than coordinated in the orthodox way to make a single, unseamed artistic event. Religious rituals, pop arts, even ordinary street and home life were seen "as theatre." A meeting took place between kinds of hyper-naturalism and the most "artificial" kinds of constructions.

Thirty years ago it would not have been possible to discuss all these categories of events "as theatre." Probably some of the categories didn't exist. Today, despite the fact that much experimental theatre activity is ended, the field remains permanently enlarged because of that activity.

Some of the most important qualities of this expanded field can be understood by looking at the theories and practice of Richard Foreman and Allan Kaprow. Foreman's writings—his plays and manifestoes—are not separable from his directing. His texts are not like those of Ibsen or Chekhov: they cannot simply be taken up by an enthusiastic director and staged. Foreman's playscripts are actually continuous with his manifestoes on one side and his *mises en scène* on the other. The manifestoes are more than concepts or proposals written down. The very arrangement of the words on paper is important to Foreman. He is writing visually; he is always working scenographically, even when composing a manifesto. As Foreman notes in his First Manifesto (April, 1972): "Always notate your exact situation and process when *writing!*" He acknowledges that "the artistic experience *must* be an ordeal to be undergone. The rhythms must be in a certain way difficult and uncongenial." Anyone who sat on the wooden bleachers in Foreman's own theatre on lower Broadway knows what Foreman is saying. In his Second Manifesto (July, 1974) Foreman outlines what he expects from himself and his audience:

The result of being awake (seeing):
    You are in two places at once (and ecstatic).
                        Duo-consciousness
    1. You see.
    2. You see yourself seeing.

The ONLY justifiable technique in art (art of this historical moment)—
The only technique which is not simply audience manipulation—
(leading the ones who sleep deeper into that sleep)
                      is
learning how to be in two places (levels, orientations, perspectives) at once.

    1) Study all kinds of "FRAMING DEVICES."
    2) Study the superimposition of DIAGRAM upon reality.[5]

In his Third Manifesto (June, 1975) Foreman names his subject: "Creativity (the effort at it) as the subject." In his own plays Foreman tries, as clearly as he can, to lay out, to make visible and bare, his own thinking process. His famous strings, frames, buzzers, and bells indicate, point to, awaken, and make highly visible under bright white light what Foreman was/is thinking. The thematics of his plays is another matter involving the cruelties expressed in male-female relationships. These themes, however, appear as the "material" rather than as the "subject" of Foreman's work. His work, along with Wilson's and some of Mabou Mines', has expanded experimental theatre to include the workings of individual consciousness as such.

Kaprow's work as one of the originators of Happenings (he coined the term) is less well known among theatre people but of equal importance to Foreman's. In his book *Assemblages, Environments, and Happenings* (1966), Kaprow lists seven "rules of thumb" concerning Happenings. He advocates keeping a fluid line between art and life; staging Happenings "over several widely spaced, sometimes moving and changing locales"; using time in ways that are "variable and discontinuous" so that "pacing will acquire an order that is determined more by the character of movements within environments than by a fixed concept of regular development and conclusion." He says that a Happening should be composed as a "collage of events," not as some Aristotelian closed structure. Kaprow also wanted to eliminate audiences altogether. "All the elements—people, space, the particular materials and character of the environment, time—can in this way be integrated. And the last shred of theatrical convention disappears." He also urged that Happenings be performed only once. Finally, Kaprow argued that "the source of themes, materials, actions, and the relationships between them are to be derived from any place or period *except* from the arts. . . . By avoiding the artistic modes there is the good chance that a new language will develop that has its own standards."[6]

Obviously Kaprow was trying very hard to stretch the boundaries of art—so much so that he denied to art any place at all in Happenings. Kaprow's ideas—some taken from Cage with whom he studied, some invented by Kaprow himself, some simply "in the air" during the '60s—bridged the worlds of visual arts, theatre, music, and popular culture. Later Kaprow became concerned with Zen and, from his California base, developed performances that were more meditations than public showings.[7] Kaprow's work did not influence Grotowski but paralleled Grotowski's move from theatre to paratheatre.

The period when Kaprow developed his ideas, and when Foreman began staging his own plays, saw conscious and programmatic attempts to stretch the limits of what performance was—to reject as narrow and restrictive the orthodox definitions of theatre, dance, music, and visual arts. Foreman's and Kaprow's work does this, but more, too. Their works are strong examples of the concern for form-in-itself: for constructing and displaying actions without communicating judgments regarding those actions. Foreman wants his audiences "to see"—to be more aware of the thought process being played out in front of them; Kaprow invents games that generate activities that do not "mean" anything in the ordinary sense—they are intentionally open to any number of interpretations. Both Foreman's and Kaprow's works emphasize process. Ironically these works lead to concerns that are mostly formal: art whose subject and object converges on itself.

Formalism, Frontalism, Nihilism

Almost without notice subject matter—content—disappeared from experimental theatre. And when it appeared it was conveyed in structures so highly formalized—like Glass's *Satyagraha* or Foreman's direction of Strauss's *Three Acts of Recognition*—that the underlying meaning of the performance served as a mere vehicle for the virtuosity displayed. At another extreme, the 1982 work of Wooster Group, *Route 1 & 9,* also produced with great virtuosity, communicated such violence as to become almost wholly nihilistic. All of these works—and I cannot emphasize enough how well they are staged, acted, conceived—were staged frontally: sequestered behind a dream-screen which if it is not the old-fashioned proscenium duplicates the proscenium's main function of keeping the audience at a physical, emotional, and conceptual distance.

Let Philip Glass's and Connie DeJong's *Satyagraha* serve as my example of a beautifully done but deeply dispirited work. Glass worked with both Mabou Mines and Robert Wilson. *Satyagraha* shows the impact of these previous associations. The opera's music is based on Asian *tala*; the staging shows Gandhi at three decisive moments in his early career. David Sterritt summarizes the action:

> Glass's opera chronicles the satyagraha struggle in South Africa, condensing the action into a single day. [. . .] Set at dawn, the first scene places Gandhi between two armies—the oppressors and their victims—and presents his determination to wage the good fight. He and his followers then build the cooperative Tolstoy Farm and take a satyagraha vow to resist their enemies. [. . .]
>
> Later, under a stormy afternoon sky, Gandhi is rescued from a mob by the wife of a local official, who unexpectedly supports his cause. Thus bolstered, he founds the radical newspaper *Indian Opinion,* and leads his followers in burning their hated registration cards. In the last act, under a starry sky, he guides his followers in resistance to a horde of contemporary policemen.[8]

These actions are staged behind a scrim. Everything appears as if in a fog; the actions unfold very slowly, implying a ritualistic significance. The language of the opera is Sanskrit, the text the *Bhagavad Gita*. Overlooking each of the three acts is a Great Figure: Tolstoy, Tagore, Martin Luther King. The opera ends with King's assassination—in slow motion. Carol Martin commented that *Satyagraha* needed something to pull itself into the present—a real gun shot, a ripped scrim, a sudden rush of movement. But, no, King is shot behind the scrim, beautifully, in the historicized past.

Gandhi made politics from religion, while Glass makes art from politics. *Satyagraha*, for all its exquisite beauty, maybe because of it, confronted me with a weird reversal. All the more maddening because from an "artistic point of view" I find it impossible to quarrel with the opera's hypnotic music, its eye-pleasing tableaux: the easy-to-look-at, easy-to-listen-to beatings and burnings. I saw *Satyagraha* in 1981 at the Brooklyn Academy of Music whose management provided buses to bring people in from, and return them to, Manhattan: the opera-goers never had to set foot on the dangerous, black Brooklyn streets. Gandhi might have had some feelings about that, but not in this opera.

Not many recent productions using the proscenium, or frontal staging, or fixed seating are graced with *Satyagraha*'s formalist beauties. Nor can many directors match Foreman's distinct and personal use of the box set which he makes narrow and deep, imposing perspective and forcing new ways of seeing. Even Foreman's use of the thrust—as in his Guthrie Theatre production of Molière's *Don Juan* and his use of the Anspacher at the Public for *Three Acts of Recognition*—gives the sense of closed, constricted movement. Most experimental theatre these days is staged frontally—and the staging is a retreat: a signal of a rejection of much of what experimental performance pioneered. To find environmental theatre staging, or audience participation, these days you must go to some of the sex theatres in New York or to restored villages and theme parks.[9]

I'm not complaining solely about the end to "audience participation." I think it is wrong to no longer see works that provide audiences with a variety of viewing angles, movement, and involvement options. For example: the way Grotowski had the spectators sit at a table while Faustus, host at his own last supper, displays scenes from his life. Or the sharing of a meal set up and sold by the performers during TPG's production of *Mother Courage*. Or the ebb and flow of a large audience moving through a vast open space as great, mobile figures hurtled through that space in Ronconi's *Orlando Furioso*. Or the intimacy of the various environments for Maria Irene Fornes' *Fefu and Her Friends*. Only Squat Theatre continues to actually play with space—getting a lot of mileage out of the storefront that is its 23rd Street performance space's back wall.[10]

Environmental theatre has been picked up—or has been developed independently—by discos, punk clubs, gay baths, sex theatres, theme parks, restored villages, wild animal parks and zoos. I think audiences stream into these apparently different kinds of experiences because in all of them a person is absorbed into a "total space" where fantasies can be safely experienced and even, in some places, acted out. These total spaces are reassuring: even the unpredictable is more or less safe. The realities proposed in such places—whether the San Diego Animal Park or the Ritz night club in Manhattan, given over to punk, performance art, and disco—are "re-creations" in both senses of the word. In many environmental clubs people go as much to be seen as to see. In some of the fanciest discos, Studio 54 for example, whole environments are constructed for one-time use only. In our own mode the sensibility of the Elizabethan Masque has been reintroduced.

In the theatre itself, even experimental theatre, things are much tamer, more boring. Even the best new work, Squat excepted, is scenographically retrograde. I emphasize scenography not only because so many innovators of the past century have been concerned with it: Craig, Stanislavski, Meyerhold, Artaud, Grotowski; but because to experiment with the space of the whole theatre, and to bring the theatrical event into the world outside the theatre building, is to investigate most directly the relationships between performers and spectators, and between theatrical events and social life. I read the retreat to frontal staging as an avoidance of dealing with these relationships.

The Six Causes for the Decline of the Avant-Garde

So that's where we are. The best of our experimental theatre is formalist, frontal, nihilistic. Many artists work as soloists. Groups have been disbanded or stay together mostly for fund-raising reasons. There are bright spots—I'll get to them later. First I need to outline the causes of the decline and explain some of these causes in detail. Not all the causes for the decline are "bad." Some are simply new situations that could not be coped with. The causes are:

1. The emergence of "performance texts" as distinct from "dramatic texts."

2. The failure to develop adequate ways of transmitting performance knowledge from one generation of theatre workers to another.

3. Dissolution of the groups and the concomitant rise of solo performing.

4. Lack of money coupled with the ways money must be raised and accounted for through applications and reports to foundations and various government agencies.

5. Stupid journalism that is often destructive of experimentation in theatre. Serious journals that have not provided enough of a forum for the development of effective leadership.

6. An end to activism in the society-at-large. This cannot be remedied by a Disarmament Movement that fails to connect arms with other social, political, and economic questions.

The Emergence of Performance Texts

From the Renaissance to our own day the main tradition in theatre has been literary. Theatre was an offshoot of drama. Drama meant plays, scripts, written texts. Rare indeed was a "great play" that was not recognized, and studied, as literature. Recently because of the impact of the period of experimentation I'm focusing on, and because of interest in dance, in the performance traditions of non-Euro-American cultures, in the popular entertainments of Euro-America, a second way of seeing performance history is emerging. This is a history not of drama, nor of the productions of the great plays, nor even the "acting styles" of the great actors, but of a very broad spectrum of "performative activities" including sports, ritual, popular entertainments, everyday face-to-face behavior, some kinds of therapy, and street demonstrations.

Always there existed a lively popular tradition of things like circus, mountebanks, vaudeville and burlesque, commedia dell'arte, street entertainers; and quasi-theatrical events such as medicine shows, magicians, itinerant singers and story-tellers; and ritual/ceremonial performances whose function was as much to entertain as to convey religious or social messages. These theatrical traditions with their performance texts were shunned academically: because they couldn't be "reliably recorded" they couldn't be included in the academic canon; they did not qualify as "high art." In most universities they still qualify only for a glance, not a close look.

Be that as it may. Theatre as it has been know in Euro-America from the Renaissance was a living event created around, and from, the armature of a play. Productions came and went, were good or bad; but plays endured. Playscripts lived double lives. First a script could be enjoyed separate from any production as a piece of literature. Plays, especially "the classics," had the status of poetry, the novel, and other genres of literature. Sometimes, as with Shakespeare, two versions of a play existed: that done on stage conforming to the theatrical conventions and expectations of the period, and that preserved in books. For more than 150 years Cordelia and Lear did not die at the end of *King Lear* but were reunited while Goneril and Regan, the wicked sisters, were punished.

Even more important than bowdlerization was the assumption that to "do theatre" meant to "stage plays." To direct in the theatre meant to know how to stage plays; to be an actor meant to know how to act in plays. Thus in a real way the development of theatre was tied to developments in playwriting. To say "the theatre is dead" meant there were "no new playwrights of note." And the tradition of playwriting depended not so much on the production of plays as on lineages of writers. In modern drama several lineages exist interacting with each other. Ibsen is linked to Strindberg, Chekhov, and a host of naturalists. Strindberg is linked both to naturalists and expressionists, as is O'Neill who owes much to Strindberg. Beckett draws on the novel, especially the work of James Joyce, and he influences Pinter who is also in debt to the French absurdists. And so on. But in the twentieth century also writers began to be deeply affected by styles of performance outside the mainstream theatre. Brecht began as an expressionist, was drawn into both the world of cabaret and of political theatre; he was also influenced by his understanding of Chinese theatre. Significantly, Brecht was as much a director as he was a writer. The absurdist line can be traced to the late nineteenth century poet Alfred Jarry and his *Ubu* plays. But behind Jarry are other nineteenth century poets and painters, and after him a very full mix from many arts. It was in fact several waves of the historical avant-garde—futurism, surrealism, dada, constructivism—that showed how performance texts could be as important as dramatic texts.

Performance texts emerged strongly in the '60s. And playwriting slipped from its place as the sole bearer of the theatrical tradition. Although critics kept looking, are still looking, for "new writers," and many special programs such as the O'Neill Center in Waterford, Connecticut, and the Office for Advanced Drama Research (OADR) at the University of Minnesota were created especially to stimulate new playwriting, first directors and then performers became theatre's "primary creators." Ellen Stewart began Café La Mama in 1962, and each night since she announced her purpose by ringing a cowbell and stating to the audience that La Mama is devoted to the art of playwriting. But increasingly over the years of its existence La Mama has become a showplace for directors and recently for groups coming from especially the Third World. The change in emphasis at La Mama over its twenty-year existence is an accurate measure of changes within the experimental theatre community. These twenty years have given America a number of fine playwrights: Shepard, van Itallie, Terry, Fornes as experimenters; Lanford Wilson, Rabe, Mamet, Guare, Fierstein as more conventional writers. But only Shepard seems authentically "major." And the line of Miller, Williams, and Albee is very distant though these writers are still alive. What are the reasons for this paucity of playwrights? Talent moves quickly these days from the low-pay of theatre to the high-pay of media. People who might have become writers became instead "auteurs"—I mean figures like Breuer, Robert Wilson, Foreman. An auteur is as responsible for creating a performance text as for making a dramatic text. And the texts an auteur makes that can be put in words does not serve easily as bases for other directors to use to make new productions. Almost anybody can stage an Ibsen or a Brecht; but who but the originators can stage a Breuer, Wilson, or Foreman?

What happened too was that the authority of theatre passed first to the director and later to the performer. People like Meyerhold and later Grotowski, the Becks, and Brook came along and said: Look the authority—the "author"—the main creator, is not necessarily the playwright but the director or the performer. The director took unto himself (and more rarely herself) the means of theatrical production. I'm conscious of the Marxist reference. Both the playwright and the producer were displaced by the director and/or the director plus the group. And the playwright, when not present during all phases of making a work: constructing the text, participating in workshops and rehearsals, was regarded as an absentee landlord: someone whose turf ought to be seized. Brecht's *Caucasian Chalk Circle* offered a model narrative: the valley belongs to those who work its soil. The writer's words were used, but his authority—his claim on the intentions of those staging the production—ceased to be regarded as absolute. Even writers working inside groups functioned on an equal basis with their colleagues. Productions thus were no longer interpretations. They were re-creations, original versions "after" or "based on" or "using the words/themes of." Often productions were collages of several texts. Grotowski worked that way; so did the Living, the Open, the Performance Group, and dozens of other groups. In this work of collage—what Lévi-Strauss calls "bricolage"[11]—the director was the center, the transmitter, of theatrical creativity: he was the new source.

I am not complaining about this shift. I was among those who pushed it. I think it is an important and positive aspect of the period's activity.

Even in groups that were supposedly collective, the authority collected around one or two people who determined the course of action for the entire group. Mostly these authorities were directors, not performers. Later, with the emergence of solo work, author-director-performer were conflated into one person. This way of working applied not only to living writers but to the dead too. Classic or rarely produced texts were raw material to be cooked over into new works. Perhaps Grotowski was the first during the '50s-'70s period to assemble work this way. His production of *Faustus* in 1962 used Marlowe's text not as a classic edifice to be entered, admired, interpreted, and hardly touched but rather as a dead body to be dismembered, analyzed, and reassembled à la Frankenstein: a "confrontation with the text," Grotowski called it. *Towards a Poor Theatre* is a collection of testimonies (in the religious as well as aesthetic sense) describing the confrontational method. This method applied not only to literature—there's a long tradition of that in the novel and poetry—but also to actor training, rehearsals, the organization of space, and audience involvement up to and including full participation.

In other words, the very basis of theatre was changed. What had rested on dramatic texts was now based on "performance texts." A performance text is the score, the total *mise en scène,* and whatever goes on beforehand to make the construction of the score possible. The emphasis in making a performance text is on systems of relationships: confrontations, or otherwise, among words, gestures, performers, space, spectators, music, light—whatever happens on stage. It is very difficult to transmit a performance text unless one establishes permanent companies performing repertories that include not only current work but works inherited from the past. This tradition is common in Asian theatre. It is common also in Western music and classic dance. But it is not the ordinary practice in Euro-American theatre.

After Grotowski almost everybody tried to work with performance texts. Some notable productions include *Frankenstein, Dionysus in 69, The Serpent,* the Marowitz *Macbeth,* the Brook *Tempest.* The list goes on and on. Terrific as many of these productions were they did not offer themselves as part of a continuing repertory. Nor did they yield a clear method. Lots of people worked at least for a little while with Grotowski; and hundreds worked with people who worked with Grotowski, and so on, until certain training methods, and methods of making "confrontational performance texts," were very widely diffused. But because these methods emphasized individual creativity, the following of impulses, the dividing up of the creative center (it often wasn't clear who was to be the director), no clear line of transmission, or method of transmitting performance texts, developed. Unlike the Stanislavski "system" or "method" no Lee Strasberg emerged against whom others could test themselves.

Also the confrontational method of developing performance texts when it worked best was founded on very strict, very rigorous body training. Too few people undertook this rigorous work when adapting the confrontational method. Instead they "followed impulses," often meaning just doing what they liked. Today only Brook devotes almost his whole effort to such work: like making *The Ik* from Colin Turnbull's ethnography *The Mountain People* or, as he is now preparing, a theatrical version of the Sanskrit epic, *Maha-bharata.*

Failure to Develop Ways of Transmitting Performance Knowledge

With the development of performance texts came the focus on "performance knowledge": training not to "do a verbal text" but to "make a performance text." The differences between dance and drama began to evaporate; movement and gesture were as important as dialogue and narrative. As I noted, Grotowski was a pioneer of performance texts and performance knowledge. He has been among the most successful in getting his ideas across. This is because he emphasized "process," specifically in the training methods he developed. These methods can be acquired only person-to-person, face-to-face. During each phase of his career—poor theatre, paratheatre, theatre of sources—Grotowski has involved people from his own Theatre Laboratory and people from the outside. From

Eugenio Barba to the latest follower of Grotowski, people have come to his work, stayed variable lengths of time, and left; taking with them their own versions of what Grotowski and his associates were doing. In his writing Grotowski proclaims a rhetoric of closedness, privacy, and intimacy—but in fact he has been extremely open and sharing. The intimacy is within the work itself, not closing off the work as a whole. (It is different in Japanese Noh drama where only certain members of certain families are entitled to acquire the "secrets.") Grotowski understands that only by means of body-to-body training can these new means of theatrical production be transmitted. No amount of writing, by itself, will do.

But how can someone like Spalding Gray transmit what he does in his monologues? The tendencies in theatre toward the personal, the private, the monological, the narcissistic grew so strong by the end of the '70s that teaching became ever more difficult. Granted that painting, especially modern painting, is also very personal. But a painting exists "forever" and those who wish to learn from it can do so. But theatre exists only in the bodies of those performing it. The difficulty is compounded by the fact that many of the best practitioners really don't like to teach. When I was president of A Bunch of Experimental Theatres of New York I tried to set up different teaching situations for member theatres.[12] People accepted the work, often grudgingly. The best thing for them was the chance to make a new piece. Teaching was definitely secondary. For Stanislavski, on the other hand, the teaching function of directing, in or out of his Studio, was a primary aim. The issue is complicated because the works being done during the period generated no "great texts" needing interpretation. Grotowski, who almost alone among those working, developed a complete and transmittable method, left theatre for paratheatre. We had no reliable techniques to pass on to young people so that they, too, could make personal performative statements, or even solo pieces.

The kind of transmission of performance knowledge I'm talking about has to be done body-to-body. We are learning better how Asian masters put the dance "into the body" by means of direct manipulation. The teacher in Bali, and elsewhere in Asia, stands behind the neophyte and moves her hands, guides her torso, pushes at her thighs and the back of her knees. This technique is still popular in Asia, though it is being challenged by the "alphabetical" method of learning a "basic grammar" as in the West. But even in the West, when performance knowledge is learned, it needs a long period of time, much longer than a three-day workshop. Three-day workshops have value as discovery, even shock; they can give a taste of what might be learned. But deep learning takes a long time.

I've transmitted what I know about directing to Elizabeth LeCompte. Through nine years of working—arguing, experimenting, seeing eye-to-eye and sometimes fiercely disagreeing—she has absorbed what I did as director of The Performance Group during the years we were both there together: 1970-1980. In 1970 she was my assistant on *Commune*. She directed a version of *Commune* when I went to India in 1971. She was a performer in *Tooth of Crime, Mother Courage, The Marilyn Project,* and *Cops,* all of which I directed. Her own directing of the Rhode Island plays overlapped her participation in the shows I directed. As with any deep relationship, there were times of conflict as well as times of harmony. But through it all we came to a special kind of respect for each other. Our contacts included much more than rehearsal and performances. This, too, is common and necessary in actually transmitting performance knowledge. The "work outside the work" is as important as the formal sessions. The deepest points of contact occurred in rehearsals and workshops, in note sessions before performances, in long discussions while walking or sitting drinking coffee. Whatever LeCompte is doing in theatre today is not an imitation of work we did together but a continuation and transformation of it.

The contacts among people in Mabou Mines has been equally deep and continuous. There is no single leader at Mabou Mines. But several key people—Breuer, Akalaitis, Maleczech, Warrilow, Raymond—interacted over a long period of time. Some have left Mines to do their own work; most still work within the framework of the Mines' association. They have influenced each other in ways that will take more than one Ph.D. dissertation to sort out.

But if a lot was accomplished during my years at TPG, a lot failed too. I can't say if the same is true of Mabou Mines, but I would guess so. There never was at TPG wholly organized teaching or research; collective work frequently came to a standstill because we were broke or fighting. From the time the Garage was first acquired n 1968 until the mid-'70s it was used only for our own work. Then in the mid-'70s lack of cash dictated a more economically feasible use of the space—we could no longer afford "dead time" just to workshop with ourselves or with students. But this "dead time" is actually theatrical pregnancy: without it experimentation aborts. And without contact with students over a long period of time there are no inheritors. We tried to bring into the Garage work we respected, but often enough, even if the work was good, members of the Group had very little contact with it. The Garage was "used" but it wasn't really generating new work.

No living tradition of experimental theatre emerged from the Garage or elsewhere. Works—some of them very good, some not so good—came and went. And so did people: they entered our world, stayed with us a while, and went on. People taught but often with less than their whole hearts. Techniques of self-discovery, theatrical versions of self-help therapies so popular in the '70s, became the main focus of actor training. Ironically these therapies took many of their ideas from earlier performer training techniques. Inward, self-appeasing experiments didn't forge any new negotiations with theatre as a public act. Theatre retreated thematically, even scenically. By the '80s the definitive mark of experimental theatre was one person alone in a small space, often manipulating tiny figures. Nor did the training techniques engender any objective body or vocal work. Such techniques were learned separately, as "skills." You studied Linklater or Feldenkrais or t'ai chi or yoga and "put it all together" yourself. But deep, effective training can be defined by its totality: it is together as you get it. The techniques people learned were either taken home or applied in pastiches none of which developed the force of a tradition. Self-discovery, in line with the "self-help" and "human growth/potential" movements and therapies of the '70s became the focus of actor training. These inward, quiet, self-appeasing techniques (and experiments) didn't force any new negotiations with theatre as a vital person-to-person oral tradition. Rather, they were taken home and kept private.

The need for whole training was still there. And this need was capitalized by those who offered quickie workshops—weekends of enlightenment sold at a very high dollar cost.

While a flourishing tradition appears to have been created for performance art—a tradition founded on music and visual arts—nothing comparable has happened in theatre itself. Stripped of its main modern qualities—story-telling, characterization, thematic content—experimental theatre was left empty: repeating routines that are by now well-known (no longer experimental) but devoid of the shock that gave them force some twenty years ago. It's as if the '60s and '70s spun off good ideas that were taken up and used outside theatre—by performance art, punk, theme parks, popular entertainments, Broadway, the regional theatre—while experimental theatre itself was an abandoned husk.

The failure to find ways to pass on what was learned to new generations of artists is evidenced in the fact that most of the leaders of today's experimental theatre are in their late 30s to their 60s and beyond—and have been leaders for ten years or more. However we may have attacked the line from Stanislavski to Boleslavski to Clurman and Strasberg and beyond such a line exists. Its existence is why this kind of naturalism is still dominant in American theatre. (Think what would have happened if Brecht had established himself here; or if the exiles from the Moscow Art Theatre had arrived with Stanislavski's "method of physical actions" instead of his psychological work.) My generation failed to develop its own means of training—of getting performance texts across to the future. For this reason alone the work of the past thirty years may prove sterile.

Dissolution of the Groups

Groups still exist—on paper at least, where some endure like bad marriages for the sake of property, reputation, and the right to apply for funds "as a non-profit corporation." Very few groups still function as groups: as collectives or associations of people who share a common vision, who work together to make a recognizable style of performing. More often individuals are straining to get away from each other—but it's a cold world out there so they stay in the group till something better comes along.

Even dreaming of collective action in a society as caught up in individual mythology, ritual, and media hype as America is, is hard. To pursue this dream of collectivity into action while making theatrical works in an environment of bruising poverty is even harder. Some communes have survived into the '80s. These are based either on economic self-sufficiency or religious fervor. The first isn't possible for theatres, and the second is an option open to relatively few people. (Once theatre and religion seemed much closer than they do today. Both theatre and religion are, in some sense, "ritual or ritualized performance genres." They are not, however, identical.) What happened to The Performance Group during my thirteen years with it is a good case in point.

From 1967 through 1975—from *Dionysus in 69* through *Mother Courage*—though many people came and went, and there was a tremendous blow-up in 1969—the basic identity of the Group was solid. A core of people, an agreement on what kind of work we were doing, and trying to perfect; consistent training, a developing body of works some of which we had the capability of doing in repertory, focused leadership. All this, including the crisis, is discussed in my *Environmental Theater*. But starting in 1975 new circumstances arose. People who were in their 20s when the Group started were in their 30s and needed to do their own work. I was seen as much as an obstacle as a help. That's because there were only so many people, so much space and time, and a very limited amount of money. Stephen Borst was the first person to do independent work inside TPG. He directed a four-person version of *The Beard* using Joan MacIntosh, Elizabeth LeCompte, James Griffiths, and Tim Shelton. Later Borst ran a workshop for gay performers. At about the same time, Gray and LeCompte began the work that led to *Sakonnet Point,* the first of the Rhode Island plays. Libby Howes joined the Group. It was LeCompte who brought her in, and Howes was more in tune with LeCompte's way of working than mine. (Howes played Swiss Cheese in *Mother Courage* during the time that Gray played the Cook; she also played Carmen in my production of *The Balcony*. Otherwise, her work was with LeCompte. She left TPG in 1981.)

Tensions increased as both LeCompte and I wanted to work with the same performers in the same space at the same time spending from the same skimpy budget. Then in 1976 the Group went to India to perform *Mother Courage*.[13] Not everyone came back at the same time. I stayed away the longest—until February 1977. When I got back LeCompte and Gray, along with Ron Vawter and Howes were deep into the Rhode Island plays.

I re-staged *Courage*—mostly to help the Group make some money—but clearly the production was tired. Group discussions in the spring of 1977 revealed that there was no new work I wanted to do that everyone in the Group wanted to do with me. I started working on Seneca's *Oedipus* collaborating with MacIntosh, Leeny Sack, and Borst from TPG and three performers from outside the Group. I'd never done that before. Aesthetically I felt the production came off, but there was something wrong in mixing people from inside and outside the Group. It was a new basis, and one that I didn't have a clear handle on. How should the "outsiders" be treated? The same in every way? Then why didn't we make them "members of" TGP? If they weren't to be treated the same, on what basis, and in what particular ways were they different? And how would this effect morale as we all worked together on a difficult production? I felt, clearly, that things were coming apart.

When *Oedipus* closed in early 1978, MacIntosh and Sack, two performers I had collaborated very closely with, left the Group. Without pause I began rehearsing *Cops,* using Group people plus Tim Shelton who returned just for this production. Meanwhile, LeCompte and Gray kept developing the Rhode Island plays. *Rumstick Road* was a great success. *Nyatt School* opened; and the work was going on for *Point Judith. Cops* was brought back for a second run in the spring of 1979. That spring I began also to run workshops with both Group and non-Group people for *The Balcony.* I staged Genet's play twice that year. First, during the summer at Connecticut College using students, Group members, and people from the spring workshop; and later in the fall of 1979 at the Garage with a professional cast that mixed Group and non-Group people. I couldn't translate my concepts into a wholly realized production.[14] There were too many tensions arising from circumstances outside *The Balcony.* Vawter as Irma, Howes as Carmen, and Gray as the Bishop were working very intensely with LeCompte on *Point Judith.* Gray was also working on his monlogues—some of which were shown at the Garage under Group auspices, and some independently produced. I felt these people were torn by conflicting, sometimes downright contradictory, demands. Borst, playing the Police Chief, had one foot out the door of TPG. After the show closed early in 1980, he left. The tensions between Group members and non-Group people, present during *Oedipus,* were rampant during *The Balcony.* There was, actually, a three-way split. There was a split in the cast of *The Balcony* between Group members and non-Group people; and there was a split within TPG between those working mainly with me and those working mainly with LeCompte.

All this was compounded and magnified by a money situation that was desperate in the extreme.

In a phrase, the Group lost its center.

Maybe TPG could have survived intact as a unified group with several centers—as Mabou Mines has survived—if a bunch of crises hadn't arrived at once: the need for members to do their own work; tensions inside TPG arising from the different ways people worked; poverty; the departure of key members—MacIntosh, Sack, Borst, technical director Bruce Rayvid—in 1978-80; LeCompte's unspoken but clearly acted upon decision not to allow the emergence of the kind of creative pluralism that has been so beneficial for Mabou Mines. It's hard for me to map a cause-and-effect system. How can I talk clearly about incompatible personalities? One thing didn't lead to another so much as a lot of things piled up. Still, all things considered, TPG—now renamed Wooster Group—has survived, and is doing important, powerful work. LeCompte, Vawter, and Dafoe are the core at the Garage. Gray joins them often while also developing his own work—he is writing fiction as well as making solo performances. Designer Jim Clayburgh also works both at the Garage and outside. Howes is gone and Kate Valk has come.

By the time *The Balcony* opened in the fall of 1979 I had decided to leave TPG. During the meetings in the spring of 1980 I almost reversed that decision. But to stay would have meant to split the Group, to get involved in a struggle with no foreseeable end. I wanted a new perspective on things. The greatest loss to TPG-Wooster when I left was continuity and along with that a chance for new growth. Under less extreme circumstances the Group would have expanded its base to allow for both LeCompte and me to work unhindered. And Gray too. As well as to encourage divergent works by other members. Something like what happened at the Moscow Art Theatre when the Studios were set up. A situation called "schismogenesis" by anthropologist Gregory Bateson. That means to grow by breaking into pieces—each piece developing in its own manner. It is very difficult to have healthy schismogenesis in today's theatre because if people leave the administrative unit that is a non-profit corporation they have a hard time raising money; and if they stay inside, few groups have found the way to accomodate divergent ways of working. At TPG I was ready to work in a studio with new people. I felt that the string of works that began with *Dionysus in 69* had run out. I wanted to find the next direction to move in. I wanted time to really experiment; and time off from business. There was no way to achieve this within TPG. Yet without this kind of schismogenetic expansion how can people develop new ideas; how can one generation's work be passed on systematically to another generation?

I know that people pick things up by simply working and moving up the ladder. I also know that special places like Mabou Mines' Re.Cher.Chez are meant as workplaces and showplaces for new experimenters. But the best way to transmit performance knowledge is to have senior people who like to teach engage in the kind of teaching that can't be done at universities the way they are administered in America now—teaching by trying out new techniques based on knowledge that's been learned over years of experience, knowledge that's in the body and has to be transmitted body-to-body over long periods of time to small, very small, groups of people. The groups promised to make this kind of time-space available. When groups began to fail, the problem of transmission of performance knowledge became insoluble.

My decision to leave TPG is not regretted. I do regret that the decision was forced on me by circumstances I believe make future growth of experimental theatre difficult. I have told my own story because I experienced it first-hand, but I believe one can generalize from the TPG situation. After all, TPG as Wooster Group has survived: it is one of the lucky groups. Other groups, for any number of reasons, but with worse results for experimentation, have failed.

Is the answer to give up professionalism? In Asia, whose theatre I admire, few traditional artists earn most of their living by performing. Many farm or do other non-theatre work. Badal Sircar, the Bengali playwright and director, has kept his Satabdi group together for many years. None of its members earn their living from Satabdi. The group's work has had a deep impact on Bengali and all-Indian theatre. Many Asian theatre artists support themselves by teaching. Teaching serves three functions: supporting the artists; transmitting performance knowledge; educating the audience. In the case of Noh drama, for example, this last is very important. A sizable proportion of Noh's audience learns the difficult conventions of the art by studying its chanting, dancing, and/or other aspects. Closer to home, Foreman divided box office among the performers but in no other way promised them a living. He maintained no regular company though some people worked with him on a number of productions. In Poland, T. Kantor works with people who get paid only when on tour. Kantor told me he wanted people who supported themselves in other ways so that they could focus on their work with him for reasons other than money. Maybe these are solutions based on necessity—but they are solutions.

At present, in America, I see no way of keeping a company on salary while doing experimental work. Yet without fulltime companies works do not enter any repertory; the techniques of experimentation get passed on only through a vague folklore of "influences." This method of diffusion is okay for painting and literature—arts where what is being transmitted exists separate from the artists who make the works. But where the art is the people—"national treasures," as the Japanese and Koreans name their great performers—methods of transmitting performance knowledge person-to-person need to be developed.

Tradition or No Tradition?

Is it, as Karen Malpede says, in an article replying to my PAJ essays, "that technique is inherently conservative since it tends to live beyond the authentic impulses from which it once was made"? And therefore:

> There is no point in teaching actors to perform in the mode of the avant-garde when what is performed no longer causes wonder in our minds. What we need instead is a serious commitment among theatreworkers to dramatic actions vital to our time: whatever techniques we then require will emerge directly from the urgency of our work.[15]

Yes, technique is inherently conservative: look at dance, both ballet and modern. I can see Martha Graham's company in *Primitive Mysteries* nearly one-half century after the dance was choreographed; and I can see ballets from even earlier times. Of course changes occur: the Graham dancers of today, I'm told, are lighter, more upper-body conscious than those who did the original dance. But there's another side to the question of technique being conservative. Using dance again as my example I can show that modern dance gave rise to—if mostly through opposition and rejection of its techniques—the aleatory and more ordinary movement vocabulary of postmodern dance. Performance history is very complicated; but in a society given to originality, as ours is, there is little danger of devotion to a technique freezing a whole genre. What's more likely to happen, as in dance, is the continuation of several parallel lines, each influencing the other. This rich exchange has not happened in theatre.

I very much enjoy watching the Jose Limon Company perform some of Doris Humphrey's dances, *The Shakers* in particular. The Limon Company is using Humphrey's original movements, though these are interpreted in a contemporary mode. I know that I am not seeing Humphrey's dance as such, but a kind of recreation of it—the continuation of a tradition which she started. I realize too that Humphrey, like Graham, was once an experimenter. I want for experimental theatre that same kind of continuity: experimentation vying with tradition. I don't agree with Malpede that pragmatism alone—"whatever technique we then require will emerge directly from the urgency of our work"—is healthy. That approach relies too much on creating the world fresh each week. I favor a dialectic between originality and tradition. In our culture: between many originalities and many traditions.

Tradition is conservative but it needn't be reactionary. To be a traditionalist doesn't mean to deny change. T.S. Eliot put it well in 1919 when he wrote:

> Yet if the only form of tradition, of handing down, consisted in following the ways of the immediate generation before us in a blind or timid adherence to its successes, 'tradition' should positively be discouraged. [. . .] Tradition is a matter of much wider significance. It cannot be inherited, and if you want it you must obtain it by great labor. It involves, in the first place, the historical sense, which we may call nearly indis-

pensable to anyone who would continue to be a poet beyond his twenty-fifth year; and the historical sense involves a perception, not only of the pastness of the past, but of its presence; the historical sense compels a man to write not merely with his own generation in his bones, but with a feeling that the whole of the literature of Europe from Homer and within it the whole literature of his own country has a simultaneous existence and composes a simultaneous order. [. . .] The existing monuments form an ideal order among themselves, which is modified by the introduction of the new (the really new) work of art among them. The existing order is complete before the new work arrives; for order to persist after the supervention of novelty, the *whole* existing order must be, if ever so slightly, altered; and so the relations, proportions, values of each work of art toward the whole are readjusted; and this is conformity between the old and the new. [. . .] The past [is] altered by the present as much as the present is directed by the past. And the poet who is aware of this will be aware of great difficulties and responsibilties.[16]

It is this sense of tradition that I seek for theatre. A sense of tradition wherein each "really new" work redefines all the works of the past and challenges all the works that are to come. Such a traditionalist viewpoint cannot be held in ignorance, generating new techniques *ad hoc*.

How does it stack up against Artaud's insistence on "no more masterpieces"?

One of the reasons for the asphyxiating atmosphere in which we live without possible escape or remedy—and in which we all share, even the most revolutionary among us—is our respect for what has been written, formulated, or painted, what has been given form, as if all expression were not at last exhausted, were not at a point where things must break apart if they are to start anew and begin afresh. [. . .] Masterpieces of the past are good for the past: they are not good for us. We have the right to say what has been said and even what has not been said in a way that belongs to us, a way that is immediate and direct, corresponding to present modes of feeling, and understandable to everyone. [. . .] What has been said is not still to be said; that an expression does not have the same value twice, does not live in two lives; that all words, once spoken, are dead and function only at the moment when they are uttered, that a form, once it has served, cannot be used again and asks only to be replaced by another, and that the theatre is the only place in the world where a gesture, once made, can never be made the same way twice.[17]

Is there such a chasm between Eliot's view and Artaud's? Granted that one writes as if from Olympus and the other as if being boiled in oil. Yet underneath the difference in rhetoric sounds a single theme: the present redefines the past just as surely as the past haunts the present. Eliot celebrates this, Artaud agonizes over it. Still Artaud does not reject technique: his love of

Balinese for their "animated hieroglyphs," their "vocabulary of gesture and mime for every circumstance of life" amply demonstrates Artaud's respect for "the deep and subtle study that has presided at the elaboration of these plays of expression, these powerful signs which give us the impression that their power has not weakened during thousands of years."[18] What Artaud rejected was the smothering of the present by an academic (literary, already known, accepted) past. What both Eliot and Artaud demand are restatements, re-presentations. Artaud saw that theatre inherently is always "original," always happening "this time only." He chose to stage Shelley's *The Cenci*, a poem already more than 100 years old, because Artaud saw in it the chance to make something new. In this sense there are no masterpieces: no work that is untouchable. That's why so much work in experimental theatre has been the *bricolage* of old texts: a process of deconstruction-reconstruction. This breaking down-building anew process is the theatre's way of doing what Eliot described.

Yet the position of experimental theatre is not yet clear. It, along with postmodern dance, stands between the "once only" of paintings and Happenings and the "performing repertory" of ballet or Asian theatre. Experimentalists reject the idea that a performance is an interpretation of a known, even classic, text; but they do not accept as an alternative the "once only" approach of Happenings. Postmodern dance will probably be absorbed into modern dance. Already works by Brown, Childs, Dean, and Cunningham are performed by their own companies with new dancers—the way Graham's and Humphrey's dances are passed on. And a new generation of postmodern dancers has emerged—people like Johanna Boyce, Dana Reitz, and Charles Moulton. For experimental theatre the problem is more difficult. Lacking a technique either to use or to forcefully reject (to react against and thereby to make something new), young experimenters wander. Imitations abound—go to Re.Cher.Chez and see them—but these imitations lack the discipline of a mastered and/or rejected technique.

In some way, experimental theatre is yearning to be dance: to have a total performance text or score. That is one reason why so many experimenters have been attracted to Asian forms that combine theatre and dance. Forms such as Noh or Kathakali represent a total knowledge of the stage, of music, of dance, of story-telling. Often they use literary texts of great sophistication. These texts are integrated into performance texts, and are often subordinate to the performance texts: to the actual ways things are accomplished on stage. The performance texts are the basis for training; training prepares performers to do the performance texts—and in this way performances are transmitted from generation to generation.

In Asia when experimentation occurs—as in the work of Badal Sircar in India, or Tadashi Suzuki and Shuji Terayama of Japan—a strong aspect of the work is its inclusion of traditional elements. Sometimes these are included negatively—as a way of blasting through what the Asians perceive as stultifying. And just as Asian modes have excited Western theatre experimenters like Brecht, Artaud, Cage, and Grotowski, so modern Western theatre has excited Asian experimenters. But in both cases technique met technique. I'm afraid what we've come to now is an absence of technique.

Without a repertory and a basic training technique we stumble into a "once only" aesthetic without consciously choosing it. Apologists argue that technique "will emerge directly from the urgency of our work." It's like saying a political program will arise from crisis. Crisis is one necessity, but an underlying vision, and a technique to express that vision, is also needed. Without vision and technique we get what we've got: bursts of energy, sometimes extremely creative, followed by sputtering inconsistency, unplanned discontinuity rationalized after the fact. If we accepted our experimental works as performance texts—doing them a few times a year in repertory instead of playing them in long runs that exhaust everyone and that finish off works forever—then, maybe, slowly, the kind of tradition of experimentation I'm arguing for would develop. A tradition to be used, transmitted, reacted against.

Solo Work—Narcissism or More?

Along with the dissolution of the groups has been the rise of solo work. The director's dominance didn't so much end as it was challenged successfully by performers who wanted "authority" themselves. As the "Autoperformance" issue of TDR (March, 1979) documents, performers like Jack Smith, Spalding Gray, Stuart Sherman, Jeff Weiss, Leeny Sack, Linda Montano, Bob Carroll, and Theodora Skipitares began to dominate the experimental theatre scene by the late '70s. Writing in the *Voice* of 20 April 1982, Julius Novick reports on the Sixth Annual Humana Festival of New American Plays held at the Actor's Theatre of Louisville.

> This is the year of the Monologue [. . .] with eighteen of them, organized into three programs, all presented on the main stage, plus several more in the teenage guest show. Has there ever been, anywhere, such a large-scale attempt to explore the possibilities of this small-scale form?

Well, before solo work went national it was the rage of experimenters in New York. I don't mean monologues in the traditional sense of a one-person show, but in the more radical sense of using the one person who is performing as the source of the material being performed.

Compressed into a single presence is author-director-performer. Roger Copeland quotes Lee Breuer's reaction to Gray's use of himself as "material" for *Rumstick Road* (not a monologue but a forerunner of Gray's monologues):

> Lee Breuer [. . .] has argued that Gray's use of himself as raw material represents a turning point in the history of acting no less significant than the innovations of Stanislavski and Brecht: "With *Rumstick Road*," Breuer writes, "it's finally all out of the bag, the statement reads: I'm my own material on all fronts—visually, vocally, historically, spiritually, psychologically, intellectually, ard emotionally. I am myself . . . This," declares Breuer, "is the third new idea about acting in this century."[19]

From naturalism to alienation-effect to autoperformance.

The concepts and practices that led to autoperformance began earlier than the mid-'70s. Gray tells how his work with The Performance Group led him to his solo work:

> Schechner emphasized the performer, making him more than, or as important as, the text. This made him very unpopular with critics and playwrights, but he was a liberator from assembly line acting techniques. The way I interpreted Schechner's theories was that I was free to do what I wanted, to be who I was, and trust that the text would give this freedom a structure. The text was like a wave I was riding, and the way I rode that wave was up to me. This was liberating for me because it allowed me to be more creative. This process seemed to work. The audience seemed to make the internal connections necessary to bring the text and actions together. There was a kind of counterpoint, or dialectic, that met in a third place, the eye of the audience. It became a creative act for them. [. . .] Ironically, it was the discovery of this personal style of working that led me away from working with Schechner and toward working more for myself.[20]

Ironically for our professional relationship but right in line with the logic of what Gray found out while doing *Commune, Tooth of Crime,* and *Mother Courage*; it was a way of working I explored as far back as *Dionysus in 69.* Gray didn't immediately do solos. He collaborated with LeCompte on the Rhode Island plays. But as that series developed from 1974 on Gray's involvement slowly diminished; he became more involved with his own solos.

In fact, the progression of Gray is particularly complete: a model of the move from actor-as-interpreter through performer-in-environmental theatre to autoperformer. Gray began his professional career in acting at the Alley Theatre in Houston. He worked briefly at several regional theatres doing roles in the orthodox manner. Some of these experiences are included as part of *Nyatt School* and in his solo, *A Personal History of the American Theatre.* In 1969 Gray joined TPG. He came into the Group suddenly, on three days' notice, to replace someone who quit as Malcolm in *Makbeth.* After that, we collaborated on a series of TPG productions, usually taking nine to fourteen months to prepare a new piece. Gray was one performer among several, but a spectacularly creative one—a person who would always come up with his own unpredictable and unimitatable way of doing things: Spalding in *Commune* quoting Moby Dick as the Manson Family went about slaughtering Sharon Tate and friends; bald-headed Hoss in *Tooth of Crime*; simpleton saint-boy scout Swiss Cheese in *Mother Courage*.

After Gray began developing the Rhode Island plays, his work with me became less intimate. We rarely worked from workshop after *Courage*. He wasn't in *Oedipus*. He attended only some of the rehearsals for *Cops* (playing Cerwicki) and *The Balcony* (as the Bishop): he really jobbed-in. His work was good, but his juices were elsewhere. Elsewhere means his work with LeCompte which drew on experiences with me, from his dancing with Kenneth King, and his hours spent improvising at the Byrd Hoffman loft. Of the Byrd Hoffman work Gray writes:

> It was there that I began to realize the power of energy fields between groups of people doing personal-abstract improvisational movement. [. . .] Up until this time I had been involved in a highly verbal theatre, but I was moving away from it and discovering what could happen within a creative, silent moment. [. . .] At last I had time for internal reflection. [. . .] I began to have a dialogue with myself. My thoughts were freer because they were not tied down to a psychological story line of a particular text. [. . .] I began to have a relationship with myself at the same time I was working off other people's energies. This was exciting and good for me. When making *Sakonnet Point* I was able to let go of a lot of thoughts about how to present a meaningful image for my audience. I was able to work more for myself and do what I pleased and I trusted the other performers to do the same.[21]

The director no longer imposed an alien order or was looked to as the source of what was done. Gray thought of LeCompte as an "outside eye"—an extension of his own consciousness. He says of working with her:

> I would bring in personal material that I was very close to—that I was passionately involved with. [. . .] Liz provided the meaningful theatrical structure. Liz had a distance on the material and could work with it without getting overly involved in the material itself. [. . .] She would take notes of what she saw each day and then read them back and tell us the actions that she liked, what seemed to work (by "work" I mean what was pleasing for her, what she enjoyed seeing) and we began to put the piece [*Rumstick Road*] together.[22]

Working this way—finding old family photos in his father's house's attic, accumulating texts from tapes Gray made interviewing his father, his mother's psychiatrist, his grandmother, and gathering stuff from the Group members' daily New York routine: records from second-hand stores, old clothes from thrift shops and defunct TPG productions, props and material lying around the theatre—and submitting all these to Le-Compte's directorial eye and ear, setting them within an environment developed by Clayburgh, and bringing everything into harmony with master tapes assembled and operated during performance by Bruce Porter, *Rumstick Road* came into existence. It was made through the process of deconstruction (Gray's and others' experiences, memories, and artifacts) and reconstruction (the technical-theatrical event on public display at the Garage).

When it became known generally that the *Rumstick* tapes were mostly used raw, with no substitution of actors' voices for those taped, and little editing, and that these tapes were broadcast without the permission of those interviewed—the voices heard in *RR* are "really those" of the "actual people"—a small scandal broke out. Was it ethical to strip people of their privacy and not even tell them it was being done? What of the unnamed psychiatrist's reputation (he makes a fool of himself)? Or Gray's father and grandmother? What of suicided Betty Gray herself? Where is the boundary between privacy and publicity in an artwork? Or in a news broadcast for that matter? Van Gogh butchering his ear and painting self-portraits? Chris Burden supervising the filming of his own woundings? These are both okay because the person making the material public is also the person creating the material out of himself. But what of the six o'clock news? Okay also because the fires, robberies, murders, and rapes are all "public acts" and those being interviewed see cameras and microphones, own TV sets, and know what's going on? What about *Sixty Minutes* or *Candid Camera*? *RR* has the grace—and I use the word knowingly—of redeeming the invasion of privacy by putting it in the service of a performer's attempt to comprehend two lives: those of Elizabeth Horton Gray and her son, Spalding. Shocking *RR* is, sensationalist it is not.

In 1979, Gray began his solo work. If his movement in TPG was from verbal-literary narrative theatre to less wordy iconographic performance, then his solos are pure person-to-person narratives of self-presentation. Gray sits behind a small table, a bottle full of water next to him (he takes small hits from it); a tape recorder too so that later he can write out what he has spoken;[23] occasionally, as in *A Personal History of the American Theatre,* a prop. But basically it's Gray and his audience, face-to-face. Gray's style in the monologues is very cool—cooler even than Johnny Carson. In fact, Gray is more like a TV talk show host, a Dick Cavett, than any stand-up comic. Except that Gray's guests are his own personae, his multiple selves. He doesn't move from the table; he doesn't impersonate.

This style got its start in *Nyatt School* which begins with Gray talking straight at the audience seated no more than three feet away about his experiences acting in *The Cocktail Party*. His solos—*Sex and Death Up to the Age* *of Fourteen, Booze, Cars, and College Girls,* India and After, A Personal History, Seven Scenes from a Family Album, Forty-Seven Beds*—were composed not by staging *tours de force* of energy as Weiss does, but through slow accumulation, sometimes by improvising in front of an audience, sometimes by writing for an hour each morning at home. In one way or another, Gray's text becomes firm, but never rigid: the tape recorder is always there at each performance to remember variations. These solos are extensions of the work with LeCompte, Vawter, and Howes. For the Rhode Island plays were collective explorations—re/memberings—of Gray's self-perceived dis/membered life. The Rhode Island plays (through *Nyatt School*), and the solos that followed them, were means of putting together through workshop and performance what the experiences of living had fragmented. The rememberings brought with them associations—fantasies, flights of imagination, connections, body-states: a way of working that has its roots in the earliest days of TPG—exercises we did relating movement, sounds, intimate recollections, and fantasies in a steady stream of acted, sung, and spoken workshop researches.[24] I used these "association exercises" both as a way of warming up and as tools for getting at material to be used in productions. With Gray and LeCompte this process was developed in its own right and taken in directions I did not foresee. That is an example of tradition, of transmission of performance knowledge, and of originality.

I detailed Gray's development because his changes are a clear example of a hard-to-describe process. There is a clear analogy between Gray's work and not only that of other soloists—Leeny Sack, Bob Carroll, Stuart Sherman, Jeff Weiss to name just those I've seen a number of times—but also to the work of Robert Wilson, Foreman, LeCompte, and Breuer: all of this work has an aspect of radical individualistic self-expression. This radical individualism gives such work its special force while dooming it often to obscurity—or at least, opacity. These artists claim for themselves the right to be as personal, as private, as painters and poets have traditionally been. But this is an art form, theatre, where most audiences see a work only once. The "innocence" of the audience urges for a popular, even simple, approach (something Brecht understood). Yet the impulses of theatre artists throughout the '70s was to make works of impressive technical accomplishment that carried multiplex messages on several channels simultaneously; and these messages—I dare not call them stories—were often both complicated and private. The Breuer/Mabou Mines' *Shaggy Dog Animation* and the Foreman Rhoda series are good examples. These works, like Gray's monologues, are meditative, self-reflexive. Gray's own work, because of its Spartan avoidance of technical means, and his own insistence on simple language, comes across clear: Gray's path toward self-transcendence is through a thicket of ever more complicated self-remembering—complicated psychologically, even metaphysically, but not theatrically; his theatrical progression is toward minimalism.

The others, by and large, have amplified their complicated thought process with an equivalently complicated theatrical apparatus. This has led Wilson to opera and Breuer to multi-media. Maybe for Breuer this phase is passing. *Prelude to Death in Venice*—extrapolated from *Shaggy Dog*—is simple enough theatrically: an actor, two phone booths, and a bunraku-like puppet who is an exact model of the actor (Bill Raymond). But the problem remains: the solo works show us an extreme personalism that is interesting enough but limited in scope. The same personalism expanded into full-blown theatrical production is obscure. Without meaning to be, such productions become elitist: not necessarily for the economic elite (though this can be said of Wilson's work) but for the artistically "in." This may be okay for Noh drama—especially since so many of the Noh audience study the art and thereby understand its techniques—but in the "democratic context" of American society elitism is not to be encouraged.

Auteurs like Wilson and Foreman don't do solos but, as I said, they adhere to the same extreme personalism as the soloists. This work is difficult to decipher but also gripping because of its quirky, inimitable originality. (The same inimitableness that makes it almost impossible to put in repertory, to be done by people other than its originators, to transmit it to new generations.) Although texts exist, along with music and designer's plans, how could someone else do Wilson's operas or Foreman's Rhoda plays or the Breuer/Mabou Mines' *Animations*? To produce these works would be like trying to dream someone else's dreams.

The personalism inherent in these works sometimes jumps the boundaries between "chosen actions" and "conditioned response." Wilson's *Dialog Curious George,* which I saw in the basement theatre at Lincoln Center's Beaumont in the summer of 1980, presented Wilson relating to Christopher Knowles (with whom he also worked in several other productions). Knowles is—according to your style of labelling—"brain damaged," "uniquely creative," "different," "non-ordinary," "special"—in any event, Knowles is not an actor in the sense of someone who portrays roles or assumes personae. He is not saying things or doing things that show him as anyone but himself. Uncomfortably, I felt the relationship of Wilson to Knowles to be loving but that between animal trainer and animal, therapist and patient, father and child. Knowles was responding to Wilson at a bio-personal level; and his responses were situated by Wilson in contexts that the audience viewed variously as funny, insightful, moving, scary. Foreman, on the other hand, is nothing but conscious of what he's doing—though the actors who work with him sometimes report that they feel like puppets—or even pigments in someone else's painting. But Foreman is knowingly projecting and constructing in his tunnel-like theatre (closed in 1979) his equally tunnel-like vision of his own interior world. We, as audience, are not seeing into Foreman's mind (anymore than we are seeing into Knowles' or Gray's); rather we are seeing the end result of a process of deconstruction-reconstruction.

Of Breuer, Bonnie Marranca has written:

> Many artists draw all their resources from themselves and continually reflect only their own image. Breuer's use of autobiography, however, goes way beyond a purely narcissistic approach; he is self-projected, not self-centered. By that I mean he situates himself in a social context, and what he writes in his plays relates to the world around him. [. . .] The use of autobiography, in the sense of the "self as text," is one of the characteristic features of current experimental theatre and performance art which in the seventies has been evolving new strategies for dealing with content. If theatre in the sixties was defined by the collaborative creation of the text, in recent years individual authorship has gained ascendency; likewise, theatre in the sixties (and all the offshoots of the Happenings, too) was outer-directed whereas now it (and performance art) is inner-directed: perhaps the shift can be said to be from the exploration of environmental space to the exploration of mental space, and from narration to documentation.[25]

Breuer's *Animations* are rich, multiplex systems. They are also opaque: hard to see through them to their innards, to their psycho-social cores. I enjoy Breuer's work too much to dump on him. Along with the directing of Le-Compte and the social consciousness, the return to narration, of JoAnne Akalaitis, his work marks out new, postmodern territory: an area where technique and content might once more join to form a unitary, powerful kind of theatre. But Breuer's work in the *Animations* did not find a clarity to match his inventiveness.

* * *

All this came about because throughout the '60s and into the '70s directors argued that performers should have direct creative access to audiences, and that part of the relationship between audiences and performers should be about the performers' actual, and often private, experiences. The source of this approach is not hard to locate. Picking up on the "rights" of artists in such fields as painting and writing, a distinction grew up between "actors" and "performers." Actors interpreted roles in the old-fashioned way. They served directors who in turn served playwrights. Performers might do acting, but they did a lot of other things too. They didn't hide their own personalities which stood out side-by-side with their characterizations, or in opposition to their characterizations. Brecht's ideas of distance fit nicely into the self-expressive painterly aesthetic imported into theatre. Integrating Brecht, Artaud, and some of what was learned from Asia and Africa, directors like Grotowski, Brook, and Schechner trained performers to be "in character" one minute and "out of character" the next. Instead of hiding offstage when out of character, performers were encouraged to show audiences their private selves as well as their prepared characters. Gray was a master of such double identifications. Exercise after exercise in workshops took Stanislavski's and Strasberg's idea of "public solitude" or "private moment" further—and brought these exercises out of workshop and into public performances. Ultimately such work was not used to help an actor portray a role or build a character, but used by performers as material to be shown directly to the public. The very process of preparation and rehearsal was made public; there were green rooms onstage and many "open rehearsals." Productions like *Dionysus in 69, Paradise Now,* and *Terminal* each played off the performers' personal selves against their theatrical roles.

Grotowski's powerfully written *Towards a Poor Theatre,* and his charismatic personal appearances, along with his productions of *Akropolis, Constant Prince,* and *Apocalypsis cum Figuris* showed Americans how technically perfect confessional theatre could be: a living example of Artaud's manifestoes. Grotowski also showed how the director, in not actually performing, but simply "appearing," was in himself a great performer. Later Kantor put himself, as director, in his own works; and Foreman, while working in lower Broadway, was often visible running the sound tapes: a performer-not-actor in the liminal space between audience and stage.

The seeds of all this were there at least 70 years ago in Meyerhold's theory of the "straight line" where the director absorbs the writer and then the performer absorbs the director, leaving the performer to face the spectators alone.[26] After 1967, Grotowski himself moved away from a theatre where productions are prepared and presented to an audience. He involved himself ever more completely in "paratheatrical" experiments that abolish the separation between performers and spectators, and with it eliminate the need for "role playing" in the ordinary theatrical sense. Once, in June 1978, in Poland, I asked Grotowski why he had "abandoned" theatre for work that I felt could be better done by therapists and people involved in the "human potential movement." I faced Grotowski and said: "You are one of the world's great theatre directors, and in your leaving theatre we have lost your impact. Others can do the paratheatrical work you are now doing; but no one else can direct as you have done." He told me that he hadn't the "heart to continue to direct plays" in the fashion that he had done. I accept that answer, even as I regret it.

So directors overthrew writers; and later, in the '70s, performers overthrew directors. What happened when performers took over from directors was that many of the basic theoretical concerns that preoccupied directors from Stanislavski through Brecht to Grotowski and Brook dropped away. People who want to perform, and who do not develop into directors of others, as Stanislavski did, are people mostly concerned with their "part." A director is concerned with the holistic nature of the production under his care. And although the two concerns overlap—or rather the director's concerns include what the performer is doing—a production is not the "sum of its parts," but an organic whole with its own logic, sometimes at odds with this or that part. A person who thinks as a performer tends to reduce the whole show to his or her part: thus solo performances of extreme personalism. It's much different to make a part into the whole than to make a whole from many parts.

Once you make a whole out of many parts—once you transcend the parts and construct a whole that is "made from" but is also "different than" its parts—you've constructed a social model. Intentionally or not you've constructed a model of the City or an alternative City. Sometimes these Cities are harmonious and sometimes fractious: there may be ritual unity or contentious dialectics at the heart of a community. But in either case the City is an arrangement, a negotiation among parts. Working in groups was an ideal practice for this kind of construction of a theatrical City-as-production. But when you have one person making a whole out of a single part you don't get fascism—because fascism is one person saying "My part is going to control all the rest." What you get is narcissism: "Everyone exists only in and through me; and me is enough." Even though fascism and narcissism sometimes look alike when they go public, they are actually very different processes. There is a strong need for, and proper place for, narcissism in theatre.

People like Gray, Sherman, Sack, Weiss, Carroll saw little need for directors as creators. They wanted directors, if at all, as "outside eyes," extensions of their own vision. Dispensing with the director as a separate creative being has been, of course, traditional in modern and postmodern dance where the principal dancer is most often also the choreographer. But dance also, usually, does not grapple with complex narrative. Though I wonder when I see such classic dances as Graham's *Primitive Mysteries*, Humphrey's *The Shakers,* and Jooss's *The Green Table.* These dances convey a great deal of social content; they are exquisite technically; and two of the choreographers also danced in the works they made. Still, what is the director's function, and can it be dispensed with?

The director shapes the *mise en scène,* selecting the events to be shown out of all the things tried—making the production, as Brecht said, out of the least rejected of all things tried: a creative, negative function. The director defines boundaries, invents rules, plays games, sorts out possibilities—first among texts and performers, later among those who work on the stage and those who work around it—designers, technicians, managers. With the decline of playwriting directors took on the additional task of ransacking literature, and/or selecting from performers' improvisations "material" (literally, the mother-lode) for narrative stuff, gestus, and dialogue.

And directors ask basic questions about theatre itself: where does it take place—in an architecturally fixed space, a found environment, a totally designed environment? What is the relationship between a production and its audience? What are the theatrical processes and how do these relate to other social processes?

As performers pushed directors aside some of these questions went unasked. Theatre slid back to orthodox solutions: the easy solutions of the "Euro-American modern tradition." Frontal staging, passive audiences, sentimental, apolitical texts. Performers tend to want an empty stage so that they can be seen more clearly; they don't want to be anyone's puppet, or feel "manipulated," so they compose much of their own material. This makes most of their work personal, and too much of it sentimental. Stretch —playing many roles very different from each other—is a goal of the mature actor; self-expression is a goal of the fulfilled performer. Away with stage effects, away with other performers, away with texts written or assembled by others. What's left is what we have in so many of the solo works: brilliant, but not enough; personalistic rather than concerned with the *polis*, the life of the City, the life of the people. Evidence rather than drama which is evidence plus reflection and analysis.

My deepest feelings about the solo and/or privatized work—the stuff of Gray, LeCompte, Weiss, Sherman, Foreman, Breuer, Wilson, Carroll, Sack—the best people around—is that their work ought to be one stream in a great river system. When this kind of personalistic work is the center of theatre something is missing. No matter how impressive the work is—and I'm swept away by much of it when I'm in the theatre—it doesn't have at its heart a heart. Let me be clear: the heart is there for the selves that are making the work; even for their associates, colleagues, family, friends. What's missing is a heart for the City as such. The work does not weep for, or be in a rage for/against, the life of the people. And no matter how we want to avoid social issues, politics, the life of the people in its collective manifestations, the City—as tragedy, satire, celebration, farce—is not only what theatre is about but its chief glory.

To a degree Carroll, Sack, and Akalaitis are attempting to make a socially conscious theatre. Even LeCompte, despite the nihilism of *Point Judith* and *Route 1 & 9*, is trying to examine the theatrical roots of the American dream illusion. Akalaitis's *Dead End Kids*, made with Mabou Mines of which she is a charter member, is a horrific farce about nuclear energy: bombs, radiation, reaction of people and governments to the seeds of the apocalypse planted among us. *Dead End Kids* begins with alchemy: the search for the means to transform "base metals" into "gold"—and this search's modern counterpart, nuclear fission and fusion. What impressed me about *Kids* was Akalaitis's ability to use the full range of postmodern theatrical techniques in the service of socially important themes. The work was not obscure, but neither was it sentimental or simple-minded. LeCompte, for her part, has moved from the personalistic concerns of the Rhode Island plays, brilliant as they were, to confronting the images of America's heartland as they are encapsulated in such works as *Our Town* and *Long Day's Journey Into Night.* In *Route 1 & 9* and *Point Judith* the idea of America, and especially the New England American family, as presented by Wilder and O'Neill, was challenged by the later, more violent, visions of LeCompte's Wooster Group (what TPG was renamed after I left). These Wooster visions themselves are informed by non-Wooster sensibilities: *Point Judith* uses the text of *Rig* by Jim Strahs and *1 & 9* incorporates a Pigmeat Markham routine and *Our Town,* not to mention Clifton Fadiman's pedantic lecture "explaining" *Our Town.*

But these more socially oriented works are the barest harbingers. Most experimental work is hung up in personalism—satisfied with quirky presentations of the creator's own sense of things, what Marranca calls the staging of "mental space." It can also be called narcissism and/or decadence. With this personalism comes a passivity, an acceptance of the City, the outer world, the world of social relations, economics, and politics, as it is. I worry about this passivity because the City is changing. If artists do not participate in the changes, do not work to make them humane, artists will end either among the victims, or, like Wilson, as pets of the very rich.

Money's At the Core of It All—Or is It?

As I chew these problems over I see how central to it all money really is.

Not just the lack of money, but the ways in which artists come into money: how government agencies and foundations make people apply, determine who gets support, who doesn't, who never even try.

Most people doing experimental theatre come from the middle class. Working class, ethnic, and racial performance and performers are segregated in two ways: by class and by ethnic or racial category. In America too often one form of segregation reinforces the other. To be poor means to be black or Hispanic or Chinese, and vice-versa. Experimental theatre, for a network of complicated reasons, not the least of which is the relationship between experimental arts and the university system, draws on the children of the middle class for most of its people. Sooner or later, for many of these people, making money counts: for nothing signals failure to the American middle class more than working hard and still not making money. And don't think there hasn't been a big brain drain. Lots of people leave theatre, or never enter the field, because the chances of earning a living are so infinitesimal. Some bright people still try to make it—especially, it seems, in experimental work. Maybe this is because people attracted to such work don't care, at first, if they earn a living or not.

For years experimental theatres lived off doles and cons. Without supplemental subsidy from unemployment insurance, experimental work in New York at least would be dead. It's easy to qualify for unemployment: an axiom of the American theatre is that 80 percent of its workers are out of work.

I know first-hand only of TPG's survival tactics. I'm sure they are typical. Even in the best of days we weren't able to pay a living wage. At most a Group member earned about $7000 a year from TPG. (All members, except me, were paid the same regardless of whether they were performers, technicians, designers, or business managers. Non-group members were either unpaid or paid according to individually negotiated fees. Sometimes, ironically, non-members got more than members: because when the squeeze was very tight members were asked to sacrifice in order to keep the Group going. I got no pay from TPG—luckily I had my professorship at NYU. Until inflation really began to rage, after 1973, this $7000 was enough. But $7000 in 1967 dollars is less than $3000 in 1982 dollars. Group members were forced to hunt for second jobs. Many lived through scam, on borrowed money, and generally moved in a halfway world where sometimes they were expected to be "members of society," even of a professional elite: appearing at conferences, serving on panels, teaching at colleges; and at other times they had to act—as the poor must—with cunning and duplicity. Good training, this, for the trickster role long associated with theatre.

Support from the National Endowment for the Arts (NEA) and the New York State Council on the Arts (NYSCA) never came close to meeting even minimum needs. By 1980 the accumulated TPG debt was over $100,000. When LeCompte became leader of the Group she brought in new managers, instituted very strict budgetary controls, and lowered the deficit in part by cutting salaries. The life of experimental theatre artists-workers in money terms at least is very nasty. In 1980-81 both NEA and NYSCA increased support for Wooster to a combined total of $80,000. A portion of the NYSCA money is now in doubt because of controversy over *Route 1 & 9* which some people think is racist.[27] $80,000—or $65,000 if the NYSCA cut goes into effect—may seem like a lot of money, but that's only because people are so used to experimental theatre getting crumbs. Compare TPG's figures to some other theatres in New York and around the country:[28]

	Operating Budget 1981	Grants and Contributions
Circle Repertory, NY	$ 850,000	$ 455,000
Manhattan Theatre Club, NY	1,290,000	540,000
Arena Stage, D.C.	3,275,000	1,148,000
Guthrie Theatre, Minn.	5,159,000	1,320,000
American Conservatory Theatre, San Francisco	7,020,000	1,525,000

Remember also that Broadway shows are routinely capitalized at more than $1 million. Movies cost up to $40 million.

Part of the economizing that LeCompte had to do meant giving up The Envelope, a second space acquired in 1978 and used for performances, workshops, scene shop, and storage. *Cops, Point Judith* (in its premiere run), Akalaitis's *Southern Exposure,* and Carroll's *The Salmon Show* were among the works done at The Envelope. The austerity measures instituted by Le-Compte have cut the debt, but she still speaks of getting a job as a waitress. Without money it's not possible to spend time in open workshop freely exploring new material. Gigs that might otherwise be turned down must be accepted making companies tour when their art might better be served by a long time at home base. Shows are kept running longer than they ought to—whenever a production earns money it must be milked dry.

Legend has it that artists "love their work" and that's why they allow themselves to be exploited. It's true that the artists themselves are the heaviest subsidizers of experimental theatre: through working for little or no pay they keep the operations going. At TPG-Wooster people work outside. Gray earns much of his income from his monologues and recently from writing; Dafoe makes movies. However nice this may be for individual development, it doesn't further group work. One of the big hopes of the '60s was to establish an experimental theatre tradition: people spending their whole lives working experimentally—as an "alternative" to both the Broadway and regional theatres. Experimental theatre, instead of being the domain of the young (before finding something "real" to do in life), was to include people of all ages. The big hope failed; TPG was reduced to share-cropping. Most of each year's grants-to-come were owed to Chemical Bank at usurious interest rates. The new policies may get Wooster out of debt but they won't provide a steady income for the performers, directors, designers, technicians, and managers.

In regard to government aid there's a cute Catch-22. The government requires that artists be paid a "living wage" otherwise a grant can't be given: anyone who doesn't pay a living wage is exploiting workers. On each year's application we listed what we hoped—prayed, wished, promised, wanted—to pay. Never could TPG pay to TPG members what was written in the application because in that case TPG would have folded in bankruptcy. Always those with "hard cash claims"—banks, printers, newspapers, hardware stores—had to be paid off the top. Software—the people working at the Garage—could wait, and did. There are still lots of salary debts owed to people: evidence of the absoute degree to which theatre workers subsidized the theatre. On paper to NEA and NYSCA things looked pretty good—$8,000 a year, above the poverty line, about one-third a New York City bus driver's salary. Here's Catch-22: this "on paper prosperity" prevented us from arguing for a big money increase in our aid to be spent entirely on salaries. "Look," government bureaucrats said, "here's what you said you would pay last year—you signed a contract to that effect.

If you failed to meet that goal it must be your fault, ineffective management or something.'' ''Ineffective managements'' are unlikely to win big increases in subsidy.

Under Reagan things won't be any better—even though the President once was, and still is, an actor. The administration has given mixed signals. In April 1982 the *New York Times* reported that the new Chairman of the NEA, Frank Hodsoll said that:

> the smaller arts institutions have the most trouble raising money. [. . .] There's no question that the National Endowment for the Arts should maintain a larger proportion of suppport for them.[29]

Still the overall budget for the NEA is being cut drastically from $143 million in 1982 to $101 million in 1983; so even a larger proportion for smaller institutions will equal less money for experimental theatre. The *New York Times,* hardly a radical journal, feels this may be the case:

> Small arts organizations and avant-garde groups, which rely heavily on Government money, appear likely to suffer most from budget cuts being proposed by the National Endowment for the Arts. In some cases they may be forced to close. [. . .] Not only will creative effort slow down in the theater, but many performing arts institutions, faced with inflated budgets, falling attendance and the Endowment cuts, say they will play it safe, relying on sure-fire box-office hits and refusing to take a chance on experimental works, which are almost always box-office failures. [. . .] A feeling that seems general around the country is expressed by Barry Hoffman, president of the International Society of Performing Arts Administrators, who said the Endowment was taking grants away from the smaller groups. The Endowment, he said, ''will keep the larger, more expensive groups going, but that will be at the expense of the experiments, of the smaller groups.''[30]

This is consistent with the Reagan program creating a class society where the poor are kept down, many as part of a permanent, despised underclass of unemployed, welfare clients, aged poor, and street people. Together with ''perpetrators of violent street crimes'' these people are classified as fundamentally anti-American: not working, not wanting to work, too old to work—useless and/or dangerous. Experimental artists and other dissidents must not expect to fare much better. The message is clear: make it, get with a big institution, get out, or starve.

One of New York's most active theatres, the Theatre for the New City, is not alone in saying it will have to cut out its street theatre program and terminate the commissioning of new works: the street stuff gets to ordinary people and new works stimulate experimentation. This is the double thrust of Reagan's policies. In dance, the NEA touring program has been cut way back. At its height 189 companies toured, in 1982 it will be 85, and the number for 1984 is expected to be lower still. Richard Goldstein of the *Village Voice* calls Hodsoll "a James Watt for the arts." Goldstein says:

> Word is beginning to reach grant recipients that major changes in the NEA's guidelines may be coming, changes that could curtail federal funding of minority arts programs, museum services to community groups, and artists whose work does not fit into formal or aesthetic categories. [. . .] Hodsoll seems bent on steering the NEA away from experimental art and educational services.[31]

This is in keeping with Reagan's policies in other areas.

What the NEA-NYSCA system, before and during Reagan, means for American theatre, and New York especially where so much experimental work is centered, is a return to the cast-a-play-at-a-time syndrome. Reduce the personnel at each theatre to the bare bones: a management and a minimal tech staff (to set up equipment and see it doesn't get stolen). Emphasize new plays—writers write for free; you don't pay one until you decide to do his/her play. Audition actors on a play-by-play basis—there is thus no costly company to support. But keep the non-profit corporation intact; and distribute press releases that make it sound like you've got a company. Such circumstances educate almost everyone to hope for a "big move"—either uptown or into TV or movies. Much of experimental theatre has been reduced to commercial theatre tryouts ("showcases") or, as in the case of the New York Shakespeare Festival, to hoping for another *Chorus Line* to support much of the rest of the operation.

Very few brave souls have bucked the tide. Ellen Stewart of La Mama is one. She keeps bringing in Third World groups, sponsoring the work of new writers, directors, and performers. But long ago she surrendered the idea of a permanent company. Only TPG-Wooster, Mabou Mines, and Squat have that. Mabou is partly subsidized by Joseph Papp's NY Shakespeare Festival. Wooster owns the Performing Garage which makes things a little easier (relatively low maintenance, some income through rentals). Squat, a group-in-exile from Budapest, has the smallest budget of all, lives in poverty over their 23rd Street theatre, and continues to create a series of extraordinary works. Charles Ludlam's Ridiculous Theatrical Company does Ludlam's plays only, building a loyal audience seeking to share in Ludlam's own style of acting and directing: a mixture of camp, literary allusion, and (mostly) gay sexual humor.

The Circle Rep, directed by Marshall Mason, uses the same actors in many of its productions but still can't be said to be a company—there are actually too many people associated with Circle for it to be a coherent company. Other production agencies—like the Manhattan Theatre Club, Playwright's Horizons, Roundabout Theatre—concentrate, like Circle, on contemporary naturalistic dramas and/or revivals of modern classics. We could use a lot more theatres like these, but none of them could be called experimental. Many have gone to the one-play-at-a-time system because it's the only economically rational way.

Criticizing the Critics

Writing about critics is not easy for me—I was/am one myself. Living in a double, or even triple, world as a director, critic, and theorist, makes me appear to be a triple agent to many people. "Whose side are you on?" people ask me. It's not a question that can be dismissed with a quip. Deep in the grain of American theatre is the prejudice that critics and artists are natural enemies; and that members of the university are still further removed from the action. The responses to my original two articles in PAJ were heated when they dealt with the critics. Listen to a few samples:

> *Matthew Maguire:* [Schechner's] opinion could damage our survival abilities by discouraging the European touring circuit. [. . .] The difficulties of fund-raising in the U.S. will become even more exaggerated if his "polemic" is accepted. [. . .] S. falls guilty of his own complaint of "stupid journalism" by his lack of exhaustive documentation and by his regressive failure of leadership.

> *Spalding Gray:* It was important what Richard wrote about the press not attempting to support or understand underground theatre in New York. I did not realize how unsupportive they were until we performed our trilogy [the Rhode Island Plays] in Amsterdam. At least three or four papers sent reviewers to all three of the pieces and wrote about them as a body of work. [. . .] The *Village Voice,* once a supportive community paper, has gone the way of the *New York Times.* We have to beg them to come "down" to see our work. It took me six phone calls to get a *Voice* critic to come see *A Personal History of the American Theatre.* [. . .] It's a sad, stupid state of affairs. A strong body of creative work cannot survive without a supportive press to at least give it coverage.

> *Ruth Maleczech:* [. . .] Remembering, projecting, inventing, screaming about money, hating the critics who keep you poor.

> *Elizabeth LeCompte:* Experimental theatre has not only lost a large part of its audience—it also lost critics who now write about political science, film, or philosophy. For a brief—deceptively brief—time in the '60s these people added their voices and ideas to the theatre. With the absence of this audience and critical support, theatre people in general are more timid—they take less risks. Bright, intelligent people don't go into theatre and don't write about it.[32]

Naturally, critics Bonnie Marranca and Erika Munk felt differently. They resisted the idea that artists should blame critics for their plight.

Marranca: Consider the relationship of avant-garde theatre and the press. If one believes, as I do, that this is a period of self-absorption, it does not come as a surprise that all of the artists who responded to Schechner addressed the subject of critics and the press. [. . .] Taken together, the replies give the impression that their authors view critics and criticism/reviewing (they are not differentiated) as a scapegoat responsible for avant-garde theatre's lack of serious attention in the culture, its financial insecurity, and all that that implies in terms of "career."

These assumptions about the role and function of critics frame the discussion unhealthily in the realm of economics, as if any commentary that does not support a work or movement jeopardizes its value in the marketplace. [. . .] The widespread competitiveness of performers and theatre groups for media coverage, and the relationship of coverage to the event and to money, should be a signal for everyone to stop and think about what "avant-garde" theatre is, and where it is heading.

If those who make theatre view writing about theatre [. . .] exclusively in terms of public relations (that is, in a way that will enhance their image and thus their monetary value) then they will have lost sight of the real value of serious, public dialogue on the art. [. . .]

Theatre artists, I think, are ignoring the real and deeper causes of their alienation, first blaming the press, then later turning to it as if it were a *deus ex machination* that could save their image and their careers.[33]

It's muddier than Marranca makes it out to be. Experimental theatre can't afford big publicity campaigns and heavy media advertising. Productions do cost money. Unhealthy as it may be, poor artists turn to relatively rich publications (forget about TV which ignores experimental art absolutely, except for an occasional glance from the public network) for "support." Support in two ways that the convenient English word means: economic aid, conceptual-emotional sustenance. This latter includes the function of communication: linking artists to their colleagues, and the theatre world to its audience. But critics too often treat experimental theatre as if it were commercial theatre. The hit-or-miss philosophy applies; works are evaluated one-at-a-time thus missing the surge and fall of an artist's developing career. Very little dialogue—give-and-take among contrasting points of view—is permitted. Often enough, as with the *Voice's* trick review of my production of *Cops* (Michael Feingold wrote as if the production were the Circle Rep's directed by Marshall Mason; many spectators went to the wrong theatre), a little joke is made at the expense of the theatre worker. John Simon is a master at using productions as pretexts for his own *bon mots.*

Erika Munk, theatre editor of the *Voice* (and former managing editor and then editor of TDR), feels strongly about what she calls the "warfare" between critics and artists.

There is a kind of warfare going on these days between the noncommercial theatre—to which I and most of this paper's disputatious theatre staff owe our essential allegiance—and critics as a group, emphatically including *Voice* critics. It's a battle that does no one any good and creates a lot of sorrow. [. . .] A few weeks ago, Elizabeth LeCompte of the Wooster Group said in *Other Stages* that a cutback in the Group's government funding was caused by reviews of *Route 1 & 9* in the *Times* and the *Voice,* and, when I said this was a completely bizarre misallocation of blame, she was furious with me as the *Voice*'s theatre editor—expecting, no doubt, that when the reviewer I had assigned came in with a carefully thought-through and honest piece I'd wield my blue pencil in censorship. [. . .] Theatres of ideas, of innovation, of freedom and depth, have become nearly as philistine about critical response as any bunch of big-money boys backing a million-dollar musical. [. . .]

The real question is that of "supportive" reviewing, which has come to mean mindlessly enthusiastic reviewing. [. . .] Ruth Maleczech (and her friends, colleagues, and supporters—including me) must know it's not the press keeping them hungry, no matter how trapped critics let themselves be in a hype-and-slash system they did not create. Critics have become scapegoats: these serious and excellent artists should be attacking the centers of money and politics instead.[34]

Munk passes the buck: I don't see the *Voice*'s theatre critics attacking "the centers of money and politics." Anyway, such Quixotic attacks on the windmills of power are irrelevant. Munk misses the point entirely concerning what artists mean by "supportive" reviewing. No one I know wants mindless praise. The *Bergen-Record* used to provide that, as did some of Manhattan's local papers. No one believes such writing: puffed-up praise is useless. What's needed is actual dialogue: debate about what theatre is, who's doing what, contending points of view: dialectics, polemics: the action that "writing about" can provide. More of what went on between Munk and LeCompte.

Part of the problem is the sheer paucity of publications. Only the *Times* among the New York dailies allocates enough space to make its theatre columns worth reading. *Soho Weekly News* is gone as of spring 1982. TDR basically does valuable but bloodless special issues. Its theatre reports attempt to be "objective documentations" of selected performances. It's not clear on what basis the selections are made. PAJ is erratic, mixing lively articles and polemics, with some very good critical material. Too often, however, the writing is turgid. And there is no clear editorial vision to go with or oppose.

What about the local papers such as *The Villager,* or the trades, *Variety* and *Show Business* or *Other Stages* which is devoted entirely to theatre and dance? What about a number of newsprint magazines like *Benzene* and *East Village Eye* where articles on theatre appear irregularly, though the editors of these offbeat journals prefer performance art? What about *LIVE* and *Alive*—again focusing mostly on performance art? Doesn't all this add up to a lot of information, a lot of intelligent disputation? No. Absent is a full critical dialogue concerning experimental performance. "Critical" is the key word here. Much of what's written is either "documentation" à la Kirby, or hype, or accounts of style more in keeping with *People* than with critical thought. And the writing is often thick as coffee grinds. I fear that Andy Warhol was right when he predicted that "in the future"—and by now that means now—everyone will be famous but just for five minutes each.

Outside New York there's very little except for California which has a lot of newsprint journals plus *High Performance* (Los Angeles) and *New Performance* (San Francisco). But, again, the problem is the lack of critical perspective. It's part of the general avoidance of content—not only narrative, which maybe we should kiss goodbye, but those meanings that can, and must, be extrapolated from events. Our culture is still numb from Vietnam, Watergate, inflation, recession. And lots of energy is burned off by sex and drugs: the willy-nilly gratification of individual appetites is an enemy of collective thought and action.

Academic journals such as *Theatre Journal* and *Modern Drama* are just that, academic; though MD is more interesting than TJ whose policy of shifting editorships every couple of years makes it impossible for the magazine to develop any direction at all. Also these journals concentrate mostly on dramatic literature and history. *Theater,* published by the Yale Drama School, has recently been more attentive to performance as such; it's getting more interesting.

But, back to New York, where the problem of criticism is even more distressing when measured against the sheer amount of theatrical activity going on. The *Voice* of 20 April 1982 lists a total of 132 productions off Broadway. Granted that most of these are lousy, it would still seem that they deserve more than a total of seven pages in the *Voice*—especially since two of those pages were taken up entirely with listings. It's symbiotic: the less attention theatre gets the worse it becomes; the worse it is the less attention it gets.

Let's return to the question of quality in criticism. The *New York Times* is a wasteland when it comes to experimental theatre. Once or twice a year the Sunday *Times* will stoop to running a feature on something experimental—usually something stylish like *Satyagraha.* But even this grudging attention is more than offset by Walter Kerr's unflagging hostility to anything beyond Broadway. The *Times*'s daily critics seem unprepared for theatre writing. Those we've had over the past decade—Clive Barnes (now writing for the *Post*), Richard Eder, Frank Rich, Mel Gussow—can't compare with the likes of John Lahr (who once wrote for the *Voice*), Harold Clurman (the *Nation*), or Kenneth Tynan. Example: Frank Rich, reviewing Chaikin's *Tourists and Refugees,* was oblivious to Chaikin's Open Theatre, or that three of *Tourists'* five performers were its alumni. Rich wrote as if the production was to be evaluated entirely on its own—one of the stupidest and most destructive of journalistic conventions. It's not even a convention that applies to reviewing books. In the *Times* Sunday Book Review most reviewers estimate new works in terms of what has gone before. For example, selecting at random from a Book Review on my desk, I can read from 4 January 1981 that "Iris Murdoch's new novel, *Nuns and Soldiers*, is an epitome and sum of its nineteen predecessors. It provides us, therefore, with an opportunity to formulate some constants among this round score of fictions and to see what they add up to." What a pleasure it would be to see this same approach taken to Chaikin or Foreman.

But those who review books are writers: the *Times* keeps a large stable to select from; the reviewers need not turn in their opinions the day after a book is published. But despite the debased and cruel circumstances of theatre reviewing dictated by box office surely the *Times* can do better. Rather than employ fulltime two or three dumbbells—and who wouldn't go bats attending theatre almost every night? A person needs to go dead in order to survive—they could have on tap a couple of dozen theatre writers each of whom would review works in their specialties: to develop for theatre what obtains for books. Why not get Robert Brustein, Richard Foreman, Maria Irene Fornes, Sam Shepard, Landford Wilson, Arthur Miller, JoAnne Akalaitis—to name just a few of the possibilities—to write regularly? What the *Times* has now corrodes groups, ensembles, collective work. It makes a tradition of experimentation impossible. It even debases Broadway, if that's possible.

And what's sauce for the *Times* should be sauce for the *Voice*.

When the *Voice* was independently owned its editors encouraged polemics and dialogue. It had the regular services of some first-class writers: John Lahr, Michael Smith, Arthur Sainer. It opened its pages to many others on a piecemeal basis. Controversial pieces were often reviewed from two or three perspectives—and with clashing opinions. No uncritical raves, but contending viewpoints. Directors and performers had their say too. The *Voice* was a community newspaper in the best sense. The community it gave voice to was of artists, political activists, intellectuals, and offbeat opinions—a kind of mirror of what Greenwich Village purported to be (but wasn't).

Since the *Voice* was bought by Rupert Murdoch (who also owns the *New York Post* and tabloids overseas) the emphasis in the paper has shifted toward commercialism. Politics and issues concerning art are still there—but ones that sell papers. Certain departments and events emerge more strongly: *Voice* Choices, Obies, the emphasis on short, snappy reviews all point to the *Voice*'s shift toward the chic. Munk tries, I think, to introduce a little sense of social context, of political consciousness—and even when I disagree with her, as I do, I respect this aspect of her editing. But the *Voice* is constricted and growing narrower month-by-month. The *Soho Weekly News,* which stopped publishing since spring 1982, tried to be an alternative to the *Voice. Soho* editors wanted their paper to be more hip, more in keeping with the neighborhood of their title. But like that neighborhood, the paper got enmeshed in questions of style—and its art policies seemed to be simply to "get behind" whatever was fashionable. It did, however, employ some thoughtful theatre critics, most notably Elinor Fuchs and James Leverett.

What about the "serious magazines"? Aside from TDR and PAJ they are mostly academic: concerned with literature, with interpretations of texts. Of TDR I have a very mixed set of feelings. TDR used to be the place for debate about performance, the place where new work was examined by means of letting the artists speak in their own words, and by presenting a welter of conflicting opinion. In the midst of this sense of continuous debate was TDR "editorial policy" usually reflected directly in the opening section called "TDR Comment." Comment dealt with any number of subjects: regional theatre, criticism, the Living Theatre's exile, Obies and anti-Obies—whatever was of current interest. Underneath it all was a consistent attempt to bring forward new and experimental work, and work that had a political consciousness. TDR was definitely international, bringing to the attention of American readers the work of Grotowski, Barba, Brook, Ronconi, and many, many others. When Michael Kirby became editor of TDR in 1971 (replacing Erika Munk who replaced me) he tried to define its purposes:

> In its inaccuracy, the name of our journal suggests some of our [. . .] preferences and aversions. *The Drama Review* has not been limited merely to drama for some time, and it will no longer be involved in "reviewing" productions. [. . .] "Reviewing" a performance means evaluating it. We are not interested in opinions and value judgments about what is "good" and what is "bad." We feel that the detailed and accurate documentation of performances is preferable and gives sufficient grounds for a reader to make his own value judgments. [. . .] We are not interested in interpretation, in the explication of "meaning," in the explanation of one thing in terms of another. These processes are subjective and personal; although they may make interesting reading, they are not very useful. There is no need for documentation or theory to be impressionistic.
>
> We would like to present material that is useful to people who actually work in theatre—material that provokes, stimulates and enriches that work.[35]

In that editorial Kirby also stated that TDR would publish writing about theatre history and performance theory.

TDR under Kirby has stuck remarkably close to the intentions he outlined more than ten years ago. And I find TDR a most valuable companion when researching specific projects. Its format of "special issues" gives much up-to-date thought on subjects like postmodern dance, autoperformance, intercultural theatre, and so on, gathered in what are, in fact, short anthologies. But I miss immediacy, the feel of combat and dialectics. Kirby's aversion to this may stem, in part at least, from his belief that criticism that is full of opinion—"value judgments" he calls it—can very much damage an artist. In his essay on postmodern dance included in Anne Livet's *Contemporary Dance* (New York: Abbeville Press, 1978) Kirby quotes at length Clive Barnes's review in 1966 of a performance given by Yvonne Rainer, David Gordon, and Steve Paxton. Barnes savaged the work of these dancers. Kirby comments:

> I would like to take the time to attack criticism in general, because criticism contains this kind of value judgment—which is extremely destructive. David Gordon gave up dancing after this review—from 1965 until 1971—and I feel he has done, since he started dancing and choreographing again, some of the most important work in the dance field in our time.

Who knows if Gordon stopped dancing because of Barnes' review? Surely stupid criticism of the kind Barnes often writes is of no use. Still I would like to know Kirby's opinions: his values are implicit in what TDR prints rather than being open for public debate. Too often when I read TDR—even the issues I myself have edited during Kirby's reign—I am left with a sense of an already historicized theatre, beyond conflicting passions.

PAJ began with a dedication to printing the "best" stuff around—an eclectic appetite for new writers, new works, the news from Europe, articles like the ones this essay is based on. Out of PAJ has spun a vital publishing industry: books, magazines, a wide range of stuff from the scholarly to the punk. What I miss, however, is a clear vision, or overview, of what the editors of PAJ want from theatre, from performance art, from all the stuff they are interested in. Maybe it's too much to ask for: I should be satisfied that Gautam Dasgupta and Bonnie Marranca scour the scene for interesting material. Still, I feel what's needed is a clear vision of what performance ought to be, of how it can function critically in society today; and through performance's prism a vision of what society ought to become—or at least one version of what it might become.

A lack of passion or clear purpose may explain, in part, the low circulation of TDR and PAJ. The editors of PAJ tell me that "anyone in theatre who reads reads PAJ." I'm not so sure. Think of the potential readership out there: 30,000 Equity members, and many more people who work in experimental theatre sans union membership—actors, directors, designers, technicians, writers, composers, dancers, choreographers, performance artists. Over the years the circulations of TDR and PAJ have evened out at about 4,000 to 6,000 each. About half that are libraries. Putting all this information together it's clear that these magazines are read by pitifully few theatre people. It's even worse when you realize that from 1960 to 1982 the number of Off and Off-Off shows in New York exploded from 19 to 132 during an average week. Extrapolating from that you can imagine the growth of small theatre nationwide (though the crest has probably been passed). And think of the audience—what droves of them don't read: not TDR, not PAJ, not anything seriously to do with theatre. Why has TDR's circulation actually dropped from a high of about 12,000 in the late '60s? Why isn't PAJ up over 10,000? Probably it signals a disinterest in the theatre—a malaise that no amount of good editing can remedy. Or it may mean that these magazines are not doing all that could be done to be indispensable journals of fact, know-how, reportage, opinion, polemic—and most urgently, far-seeing vision.

The End to Activism: The Road to Nihilism and Formalism

Matthew Maguire began his response to my PAJ articles this way: "There is something out there so coiled, so electric, so hot, I can smell the air burning. It's a presence." Maybe in the Bronx, or El Salvador, or Lebanon, or wherever the latest crisis is, but not in the theatre. And not in people's responses to social crisis either. Except for the movement against nuclear arms, the masses of Americans may be sullen, unhappy, but they are calm, even passive. The ingredients for the "burning air" Maguire smells are there: unemployment in the millions, a terribly unfair distribution of wealth and power, a disenfranchised underclass, racism, sexism. But except for the angry message implicit in street crime there are no manifestations of widespread unrest—no feeling of rebellion, let alone revolution. The middle class is in power, its rallying cries being: "Build more prisons! Clean up the streets!"

Dirty streets littered with people. The misery of some in New York is so obvious that the city has become another Calcutta. In my neighborhood dozens of street people sleep in doorways, lie sprawled on the benches of Pennsylvania Station, wander the side streets. Many beggars; many persons sick with open sores; many barefoot and bleeding in midtown Manhattan; many stoned on alcohol and drugs. Passersby, me included, step over the fallen: humans we have learned to treat like offensive, unsightly garbage. Will some truck come by one night and clean these people out of the streets? Of course I am angry at myself for neglecting these people. But I am not Viridiana, the cinema-saint who took the homeless in (until they took over her home); nor is there in New York a Mother Theresa whose Calcutta "Home for the Destitute Dying" focused attention on that great city's street people. What's needed, finally, is not individual charity but a change in social order.

Around America there are thousands of grass roots organizations, the outcome of the last period of general unrest from the mid-'60s to early '70s. Local organization, but no society-wide movement that can lead to a consensus powerful enough to effect national policy.

The movement against nuclear arms is an exception. But its program is so acceptable, its base so broad, that I doubt it will lead to structural changes in the American social, political, or economic order. Everyone is against being blown to kingdom-come by nuclear weapons. No one has yet forced people to see links between overall military policy including Defense Department spending as a whole, the ways big business works, the misery of so many poor and underclass people caused by the termination of social action programs, and nuclear arms. To force these links would be to "politicize" the anti-nuclear movement—something its leaders are working hard to avoid. But without politicization, and the hard struggle and divisions of purpose it implies, I fear that the anti-nuclear movement will win all its points rhetorically while not actually accomplishing the abolition of nuclear arms.

Clearly, experimental theatre is very far from even noticing these issues. There are exceptions. The Bread and Puppet bravely marches; Akalaitis's *Dead End Kids* addresses the nuclear question directly; Leeny Sack's solo *The Survivor and the Translator* recollects in a personal and immediate way Sack's version of Sack's grandmother's experiences in the Holocaust; Bob Carroll deals with ecology, including nuclear and big business pollution, in *Salmon Show*. But mostly theatre is locked into its formalist or personalistic box. Maguire is worried about the survival of experimental theatre. But to do what? To say what? He names a lot of people and groups. He dwells on the dismal economics of theatre. But the only vision he offers is:

> The avant-garde in the '80s is not primarily concerned with what is "new" but rather is developing those concepts that surfaced in the first third of the century and have been submerged in the middle third. The concepts of the Bauhaus, the Futurists, the Constructivists, the Surrealists, like speed, the meshing of media, the horizons of technology, the redefinition of what the artist may do. The time is self-absorbed, spinning back on itself, whirls and eddies, a vortex. We must contain more and more, we are consuming the century. [. . .] The artist well suited to this time is close to Robert Fripp's concept of "small intelligent mobile units," the solo artist; dense conceptually, survival oriented, ready to perform and tour at a moment's notice, characterized by a disdain of imitation/the misquotation of reality.[36]

This is a formalist manifesto, with a touch of sci-fi.

Maguire is worried about funding—he fears that my analysis of the decline of the avant-garde will negatively effect money-givers. Are his small intelligent mobile units of artists to be paid for by the National Endowment for the Arts? Are these units ready for "accountability?" That means application forms, self-justifications translated in bureaucratic jargon, audits sanctified by Certified Public Accountants, interviews with middle level officials whose offices smell of polyester, panels of peers (so-called), and lots of unholy alliances with the likes of Mobil Oil. Are Maguire's mobile units' readiness to tour at a moment's notice to be programmed into some big booking agent's computers? If all this is so, it is the outcome of a cruel decade where at first, through government money, experimenters were offered a small desk in an anteroom of the establishment. Steadily artists whose ideology put them outside, as Maguire's does, lost their status as outsiders—but they never gained status inside. In the process of being pushed around—benevolently, understand, always with a little loose change from the dole—these artists lost their social purpose. The outcome is Maguire's weird complaint. He wants to be survival oriented on public money.

Unlike Renaissance artists who were out front required to celebrate their patrons—a situation that obtained to a degree in the '30s—the NEA artists were always encouraged to be "free," but also to fill in the forms neatly, not to offend whatever was broadly interpreted as the "public good." Implicitly the contradiction took root: How to be against the government when the government is the main source of support? How to oppose the military-industrial complex (first so called by General and President Dwight D. Eisenhower, remember?), or the multinationals, when these were the main alternative sources of money? How to despise the richness of the rich when these people were still another source? The most manifest symptom of these contradictions was the abandonment of content. I'm not surprised that in Maguire's vision the time is self-absorbed, spinning back on itself, whirls and eddies, a vortex.

That's the problem.

The intense social activity of the '50s through early '70s was based on two main issues: the determined movement of blacks, joined at the time by many whites later vilified as "liberals," and starting in the '60s the campaign against the war in Vietnam. These movements shared a common vision of established government, economic policies, and the ways power was gotten and kept in America. As such the Freedom and Anti-war movements were profoundly radical. They stirred up millions of people—but they also scared millions more. With the onslaught of the oil crisis of the mid-'70s, and with it the first of several deep recessions; and with the end of the Vietnam War—a messy ending with no clear cut American disengagement, just a helter-skelter evacuation (we still do not have diplomatic relations with Vietnam—but recall how quickly things were normalized after World War II with Germany and Japan)—the mood of middle class America changed. Blacks were a threat on the economic front—if there weren't enough jobs let the blacks wait; resegregation crystallized very swiftly, implicit in it all the classic forms of racism. Radicals were reintegrated when they gave up their childish pursuits and became "constructive," as Abbie Hoffman did. Others were just crazies and went underground where "naturally" they turned to "terrorist violence." Quickly the utopian activism of the earlier period became bitter and cynical. It is no accident that LeCompte regards the world around her nihilistically; or that many other artists retreat into a formalist order.

"I Can't Go On Like This. [. . .] Well? Shall We Go?"

Bleak. A theatre without a new generation of young people. A set of stars—Chaikin, Foreman, Wilson, Breuer, et. al.—who have been fixed as Polaris for more than ten years. An uninformed, trivializing press; serious journals either frozen or adrift. No leaders defining what theatre is, arguing for what it ought to be. Big talents being drawn down into the black holes of formalism and nihilism. Subsidy so inadequate that it forces good people out of theatre and discourages young people from entering. Those who do enter are hopeless before they begin: they want to make it on soaps, get a few commercials, find a snug harbor in some regional theatre. Many want to become part of the star-making machine to be processed through showcases for export to TV and movies. Make no mistake about it: TV and movies are creative mostly for directors, not performers.

Failing to find ways to transmit performance knowledge means that four generations (as theatre movements are reckoned) after Cage, three after Malina and Beck, two after Chaikin, Breuer, Akalaitis, Foreman, and Wilson, one after LeCompte, Sherman, and Gray there is—who? There are young people working, but they don't cohere as a group, or a movement; or as a set of groups or movements. Is the very brilliant work of the past thirty years to be finally regarded as sterile? No one has found a way to transmit multiplex, total theatrical texts. No one has made a living tradition from what people in the period under consideration wrought. Although many artists have taught, usually as a way to keep the wolves from the door, few found satisfaction in their teaching. This meant there were few students—few followers who had systematic training in experimental theatre. I know only of the program Jerry Rojo directs at the University of Connecticut and New York University's Experimental Theatre Wing directed by Ron Argelander. Otherwise the formal training in experimental theatre is left to pot luck.

What a way to treat a detailed system of "research" developed over more than three decades of intense work. A system that involves the gathering of materials from many sources, working through everything during workshops, integrating objective outside stuff with self-generated, sometimes very personal inside stuff—combining items as divergent as scientific treatises with the intimate associations of performers—and ultimately submitting all this material to a rigorous rehearsal process.

In terms of production, the Akalaitis *Dead End Kids,* imperfect as it is, offers a model not only of the experimental system of making a performance but also of a politically conscious end-product. *Dead End Kids* uses the full range of experimental theatre techniques in the service of investigating—through farce, nightmare, documentary, and irony—the nuclear question. The problem is situated as one that comes from the transformation of medieval values into those of the humanist epoch: the quest for absolute knowledge—the Faustian bargain with the devil. From there the production branches out into numerous possibilities. *Dead End Kids* says, in its own very theatrical way, that human survival depends on building up human values. Whether or not this society, or any other, does this building up is a matter of choice. I say "building up" because in the rush to explore techniques, and to be self-referential, many have left behind the ethical dimension of theatre. It is time to reclaim, to reinvestigate, this ethical dimension—without abandoning the breadth and complexities of our new techniques. It is time to make an experimental political theatre.

* * *

Where do I see bright spots? Do I have to see bright spots?

The work of the "old masters" is masterful. What a pleasure to watch a mature Breuer or Foreman work.

Also, clearly, the experiments of the past decades have expanded the range of what theatre workers, and the public, accept as theatre. Postmodern information theory has been absorbed into performance. Performance events weave strands of media, live performers, texts, source materials, and so on, together in a braid that is not necessarily dominated by words or any other single element. Our resources, and powers, have thus been much enlarged. Some handle electronic media as naturally as earlier generations sewed costumes. Having freed themselves from playwrights, and later from directors, many performers have made new connections to dancers, musicians, filmmakers, visual artists, novelists, poets, and non-fiction writers. In this global use of what's available they are like performers in Asia, Africa, and Native America. With this critical difference: non-Western master performers are often at the very center of their cultures. Because of what I call our lack of ethics Euro-American performers are still on the fringe. (It is an irony, not a contradiction, that Reagan is an actor.) No longer the raging fringe of the historical avant-garde; not yet respected and feared like a band of Tiresiases.

And then there is interculturalism—a theme I've presented in several writings.[37] The world seems to be learning how to pass from its national phase to its cultural phase: the markers that are increasingly meaningful are not those that distinguish nations but those that distinguish cultures. If nations defend their boundaries, cultures have always been promiscuous, and happily so. For hundreds of years Euro-American popular theatre, music, and dance have been under the influence of African performance; more recently Asian performance genres have gained in importance here. The music of John Cage and Philip Glass, the bunraku-like puppets of Mabou Mines' *Shaggy Dog Animation*, the giant masks that Julie Taymor makes, Islene Pinder's Balinese American Dance Theatre—these are just a very few examples that spring quickly to mind. Asian thought is very present in the California consciousness—whether it be expressed in the "human potential movement," consciousness raising, Anna Halprin's dance-rituals (which influenced the people who made the Judson Dance Theatre, and through them the postmodern movement in dance), or the recent Happenings of Allan Kaprow. Certainly in Europe interculturalism in theatre is growing, as witnessed by Grotowski's Theatre of Sources and Barba's center for "theatre anthropology."

At a fundamental level interculturalism operates in the postmodern world. I mean: peoples are going to have to learn to be intercultural if our species, and many of our sister species, are to survive. Clearly nationalism, and its rivalries, armaments, boundaries—culminating in the nuclear catastrophe of mass extinction—is something we humans are going to have to learn to get rid of. Learn to be intercultural? More like unlearn what is blocking us from returning to the intercultural. For as far back as we can look in human history people have been deeply, continuously, unashamedly intercultural. Borrowing is natural to our species. The swift adoption of Western technology by non-Western peoples is only a recent example of very ancient patterns of acculturation. What is borrowed is swiftly transformed into native stuff—at the very same time as the borrowing re-makes native culture. So human cultures—the most traditional even—when viewed holistically, are something like the earth viewed from near-space: a whirling mass of constantly changing patterns, incorporating what is introduced, sending out feelers into the surround: very active, yet very well organized. Syncretism and the making of new cultural stuff is the norm of human activity.

Only with the advent of a particularly virulent form of Western Euro-American exploitative nationalism, and its ideological outgrowths (including Soviet Marxism), was interculturalism foreclosed. We must work to make this foreclosure temporary. Thus, I am arguing for both an experiment and a return to traditional, even ancient, values. This argument has been implicit in experimental art for a long time: it is the root of that art's "primitivism." Interculturalism is a predictable, even inevitable, outcome of the avant-garde—its natural heir.

As systems of communication and transportation—information systems actually—grow more flexible, people will be able to adopt "cultures of choice" in addition to their cultures of birth. Some very contemporary modes of cultural exchange—such as tourism, and the tours of theatre groups—are going to be included in "serious" thinking, and not just as negatives. We think nothing of eating Thai food one day, northern Italian the next, and Japanese the next. This is not "unnatural," but part of the expected benefits of cosmopolitan life. The time is coming when people will practice each other's cultures the way some people now learn second, or third, languages.

I'm not Pollyanna about all this. Values collide, sometimes with terrible outcomes. And some very sinister forces are present in interculturalism. First off, it is people from the economically advantaged places that are able to travel and import. Areas are culturally advantaged because of extensive and long-term exploitation of other areas. Many tourists, as well as some impresarios exporting and importing performances, are Philistines or worse. Also multinational corporations who seem to be succeeding the nations as the Princes of the Earth are not any better equipped ethically than their predecessors in government. I trust not Exxon. The multinational network has only one advantage: it is not in these conglomerates' self-interest to promote, or permit, global war. Still, as we unhappily see each month, "small wars," as well as the arms industry, still make good business.

I am opposed to trends toward one world under the aegis of state capitalism, corporatism, or international socialism. But I am opposed, too, to the national and ideological fervor that has led us to the edge of nuclear annihilation—and that has pushed us over the edge of squandering energy, wealth, and resources—human and non-human—on death industries.

So where does that leave me? And where do I think it leaves the theatre? I am in dialogue with some like-thinking people, mostly anthropologists and performance specialists: Victor and Edie Turner, Barbara Myerhoff, Phillip Zarrilli, John Emigh, Alfonso Ortiz, Masao Yamaguchi, Jerome Rothenberg, and others, who can help give theatre people a broadened view of performance—of how ritual and popular and art performances affect people, and what functions performance might fulfill across a broad spectrum including entertainment, social action, education, and healing. Concepts of shamanism, performance theory, and social drama have joined my earlier awareness of orthodox and experimental theatre.

I don't think this expanded awareness will lead to political theatre in the Brechtian or Living Theatre sense. Theatre doesn't "do" politics anymore than it "does" ordinary life or ritual. Each of these processes—ritual, ordinary life, politics—stands side-by-side with the theatrical process. One of the truly fine things to come from the high-energy experimental period now ended is the recognition that theatricality is among the primary human activities. It is not a mirror, but something basic in itself. Theatricality doesn't imitate or derive from other human social behavior, but exists side-by-side with them in a weave. Theatre doesn't do politics as Beck and Malina think; it doesn't do ordinary behavior as Stanislavski and Strasberg thought; it doesn't do ritual as Grotowski believed in his "Holiday" phase. Theatricality is a process braided into these other processes. It is our job—and here I am polemical on behalf of the future I want to bring into being—to investigate the multiplex weaves we can obtain by braiding these basic human social behaviors. The same event can be political, ordinary, ritualized, and theatrical.

The future is always coming out of crisis in the most literal sense—for "crisis" means fork or division: choices made. For every path taken a universe of pathways is left behind. The path of interculturalism I am urging is one which weaves together many of the threads of experimental theatre of the past thirty years. But there are other paths, and I don't want to foreclose them. The world is big enough for genuine pluralism.

During the hard cold of January 1981 I met a man of around thirty at the intersection of Washington Place and Broadway. I knew him from the time he was a student of acting at the NYU School of the Arts, and before, while he was studying Kathakali at the Kalamandalam in Kerala. He's a fine performer trained in two traditions. "Whatchya been doing?" I asked. "Oh, hustling for jobs—commercials, showcases, things like that." "How do you eat?" "Carpentry." For two years since he finished at NYU that's been his life. I suggested to him that maybe what he could do was find a few like-minded people and start a group, a cell, a club. "What kind of art would you have made," I asked him, "if for these two years you used your carpenter's skills to subsidize your theatre instead of your hustle?" "I dunno," he said, "it's worth thinking about." And he pedaled his old ten-speed on down Broadway.

In Noh drama the lifted foot about to stamp on the highly polished, resonant wood stage is Mu. The art is to hold the foot up just long enough. Mu is pure pregnancy, the womb, potentiality, ground, *unwelt,* chaos in its naked sense of gaping all-promising space. Such chaos is the domain of those sacred clowns who do everything backwards: creating anti-structure not only to delimit the domain of what is but to open to the universes of what Stanislavski called the "as if." We have passed from our period of intense activity into our Mu.

Footnotes:

[1]Matei Calinescu, "Avant-Garde, Neo-Avant-Garde, Postmodernism: From Negation to Dialogue," unpublished manuscript.

[2]The organizers of The Gathering are members of the Cherry Creek Theatre of St. Peter, Minnesota. They publish *Theaterwork,* first a newspaper, but, commencing with the May - June 1982 issue, a magazine. The table of contents of this issue includes essays about the Cuban Teatro Nuevo's visit to the U.S., "Techniques as Message," which is "part of a series on process," and reports on various "progressive theatre" activities around the country, including preparations for the June 1982 Disarmament Demonstrations. The September/De-

cember 1981 issue included a special section on The Gathering. Attendance at The Gathering was not limited to theatre people. A number of anthropologists, journalists, and non-theatre writers also were there. Kind of comparable to The Gathering was the annual "August Moon" celebrations sponsored by the Iowa Theatre Lab (Ric Zank) now permanently in residence in Catskill, New York. The difference is that August Moon drew mostly "alternative theatre" people; it didn't have the grass roots, populist, leftist quality of The Gathering. I use the past tense because, as best I know, August Moon is no more.

[3] It's really very hard to tell how many experimental, or alternative, theatres there were, or are. Theatre Communications Group publishes its *Theatre Profiles* with a national list; *Theaterwork* has its list; the Off-off Broadway Alliance has its list; theatre associations in San Francisco and Los Angeles have their lists. But many groups aren't on the lists. I get the feeling that the number of groups is in the many hundreds, maybe thousands; and that this number has increased markedly over time. Many of these theatres are not fulltime professional theatres. But neither are they "community theatres" in the middle-aged ladies, amateur sense. They are a new breed. How hardy remains to be seen.

[4] Eugenio Barba, possibly the most active experimentalist in Europe at this time, has picked up on lots of Grotowski's ideas and put them powerfully into action. One of these was implicit in Theatre of Sources where master teachers-performers from different cultures were brought together for an extended period of time (weeks-months) to exchange techniques with each other and with visitors. A kind of "global village" of performance was established. What UNESCO's Theatre of Nations does at the level of finished performances, Theatre of Sources, and later Barba's Institute for the Study of Theatre Anthropology, did at the level of training. Barba reports on ISTA's activities in the "Intercultural Performance" issue of TDR, which I edited, Vol. 26, No. 2 (T94), Summer, 1982: 5-32.

[5] From *Richard Foreman Plays and Manifestos,* edited by Kate Davy, New York University Press, 1976.

[6] There is no pagination for *Assemblages.* The essay which I'm quoting from occurs in the center of the book.

[7] See, for example, Kaprow's description *Team,* published in *High Performance,* volume 3, double no. 3/4, Fall/Winter 1980: 54-44. California art is most interesting with regard to the development of a consciousness and technique often more Pacific than Atlantic oriented, more facing toward Asia than Europe. See *Performance Anthology: Sourcebook for a Decade of California Performance Art,* editors Carl E. Loeffler and Darline Tong, San Francisco: Contemporary Arts Press, 1980.

[8] From Sterritt's review in *The Christian Science Monitor,* 31 August 1981.

[9] For a more detailed discussion of restored villages and allied kinds of performance environments and behaviors, see my "Restoration of Behavior," *Studies in Visual Communication,* Vol. 7, No. 3: 2-45.

[10] See my "The Natural/Artifical Controversy Renewed" in this book. Squat is a truly experimental theatre, and a very good one. I do not discuss its work in detail in this essay because Squat is essentially a European theatre living in exile in New York. I wanted to concentrate here on the American avant-garde.

[11] Lévi-Strauss first used this word in an anthropological way in *The Savage Mind,* University of Chicago Press, 1966. L-S explains that *bricolage* is the ability to make structures that radiate meaning based not on what a thing is so much as from the new relationships among its parts. "The 'bricoleur' is adept at performing a large number of diverse tasks. [. . .] His universe of instruments is closed and the rules of his game are always to make do with 'whatever is at hand,' that is to say with a set of tools and materials which is always finite and is also heterogeneous because what it contains bears no relation to the current project, or indeed to any particular project, but is the contingent result of all the occasions there have been to renew or enrich the stock or to maintain it with remains of previous constructions or destructions" (17). L-S says that "mythic thought"—which he prefers to call "prior" rather than "primitive"—is *bricolage.* In many ways, so is art, especially theatre where so much material—human and otherwise—is used because it is "at hand." I am reminded of Brecht's terse advice

to directors: "You want to build a house? Use the bricks that are there."

[12]In the mid-'70s The Performance Group, Mabou Mines, Foreman's Ontological-Hysteric Theatre, Ludlam's Ridiculous Theatrical Company, Section 10 (later a woman's group, The Cutting Edge), Manhattan Project (Andre Gregory), and Meredith Monk-The House formed a collective designed to streamline business operations, obtain bookings and joint appearances, and promote artistic exchanges among member groups. Mercedes (Chiquita) Gregory was the administrator of The Bunch, I was its first president, succeeded by Richard Foreman, who I then succeeded. The Bunch achieved many of its goals, but only up to a limited point. Bookings were obtained, joint residencies, especially during the summers at Connecticut College in association with the dance festival there, happened. At meetings a very lively bunch of people (not only directors but every individual member of each company was invited, and often enough thirty or more people were at meetings) met—but most of the talk was about business, and the lack of money. Some exchange of ideas rubbed off, and it was usually fun to get together; but the deep, ongoing dialogue many people wanted to happen didn't.

[13]An account of TPG's tour through India from February to April 1976 is given in my "The Performance Group in India," *Quarterly Journal of the National Centre for the Performing Arts* (Bombay), Vol. V, No. 4, December 1976: 9-28.

[14]See my "Genet's *The Balcony:* A 1981 Perspective on a 1979/80 Production," in *Modern Drama,* Vol. XXV, No. 1, March 1982: 82-104.

[15] Karen Malpede, "Tending the Avant-Garden: Can Feminism Save Avant-Garde Theater?" *Soho Weekly News,* 13 October 1981: 18.

[16]T.S. Eliot, "Tradition and the Individual Talent," in *Selected Essays,* London: Faber and Faber, 1953: 14-15.

[17]Antonin Artaud, "No More Masterpieces," in *The Theater and Its Double,* New York: Grove Press, 1958: 74-5.

[18]Ibid., "On the Balinese Theater," 55.

[19]Roger Copeland, *New York Times,* Arts & Leisure Section, 3 June 1979: 1, continued on 20-21. Copeland is complaining about the narcissistic tendencies in American theatre. I share many of his worries.

[20] Spalding Gray, "About *Three Places in Rhode Island,*" TDR, Vol. 23, No. 1 (T81), March 1979: 32-3.

[21]Spalding Gray, "Playwright's Notes," *Performing Arts Journal,* Vol. III, No. 2, Fall 1978: 87-88.

[22]Ibid., 88.

[23]Gray is moving more and more toward writing. He is currently working on a novel. His monologue *Seven Scenes from a Family Album,* New York, Benzene Editions, 1981, was written out before it was spoken.

[24]Detailed descriptions of this kind of exercise are provided in my *Environmental Theater,* New York: Hawthorne Books, 1973.

[25]Bonnie Marranca, "The Self as Text," PAJ 10/11 (*Performing Arts Journal,* Vol. IV, No. 1/2), double number, 1979: 85-6.

[26]See Meyerhold's "First Attempts at a Stylized Theatre" in *Meyerhold on Theatre,* translated and edited by Edward Braun, New York: Hill and Wang, 1969: 49-58, but especially 50-51. This essay of Meyerhold's was written in 1907.

[27]In a memo from Rob Marx, NYSCA Theatre Staff to Mary Hays, director of NYSCA's Theatre Section, dated 12/18/81 Marx said: "The consensus of opinion throughout the Council process was that the Group's production of *Route 1 & 9* contained in its blackface sequences harsh and caricatured portrayals of a racial minority. Among the examples cited was the production's use of live telephone calls: white actors in blackface call local fried chicken outlets and while using a broad mimic of Black dialect attempt to place orders for delivery at the theatre. [. . .] We also discussed the general context of the blackface sequences, the possi-

bility of a gap between the Group's intent and the reality of the production on stage, the range of interpretations, and how these interpretive elements fall within the Council's analytical concerns for artistic quality and public service. We explained that because of its negative assessment of *Route 1 & 9* in terms of these issues, the Council found it inappropriate to support the production with NYSCA funds that are raised as taxes from the community at large in New York State.'' The Council's decision is still under appeal as I write this. At two panel discussions concerning *1 & 9* held at the Garage the audience was split concerning the production's use of blackface. Most blacks who spoke were very opposed to it; most arttists—Richard Foreman and Lee Breuer among them—thought the production very strong. If it was racist, said Breuer, then it's anti-white racism: because the performance exposed white attitudes very clearly. Of course, *1 & 9* is about more than its black-face section which is offensive to blacks if taken out of context. It remains offensive within the context of the whole production, but not particularly to blacks. What *1 & 9* shows is a range of middle class white attitudes stripped to their nihilistic, racist, and sentimental bone. What LeCompte & Company do to Pigmeat Markham they also do to Clifton Fadiman, Thornton Wilder, and LeCompte's own home town.

[28]This information was provided to me by the staff of the Theatre Communications Group.

[29]Reported by Susan Heller Anderson, *New York Times*, 24 April 1982.

[30]*New York Times*, 19 February 1982, in an article that begins on page 1.

[31]*Village Voice*, 10-16 February 1982: 47.

[32]All of these statements are from a special section in PAJ devoted to responses to my original two articles. See "The Decline and Fall of the (American) Avant-garde Part III—The Responses," PAJ 16 (*Performing Arts Journal*, Vol. VI, No. 1), 1981: 38-67.

[33]Ibid., 43.

[34]*Village Voice*, 23 February-1 March 1982: 84.

[35]TDR, Vol. 15, No. 3A (T51), Summer 1971: 5-6.

[36]PAJ 16, Vol. VI, No. 1, 1981: 43.

[37]See the "End of Humanism" and "Crash of Performative Circumstances" in this book. Also the Intercultural Performance issue of TDR, Vol. 26, No. 2 (T94), Summer, 1982, which I edited.

THE NATURAL/ARTIFICIAL CONTROVERSY RENEWED

The
Natural/Artificial
Controversy
Renewed

The basic problem (for here and now). Where does "natural" life leave off and "artificial" life begin, and what's it got to do with theatre? There's an old argument in theatre between people who think the actor is better off feeling the actual emotions of the character he's portraying and others who think the actor should work "technically," to evoke responses within the audience but not to himself succumb: after all, who can *be* Hamlet eight times a week? One solution is to perform only occasionally, not as a function of the assembly line but when the spirit moves, as with shamanic performances, or even (sometimes) the work of Grotowski's Polish Lab. But the natural/artificial question is pertinent not only to art but even more to society because the planet is now almost totally webbed in communications systems = artificiality.

What's wild is in reservations, and these include states of mind: doubt ("I have reservations about that"), special time/spaces ("I have a reservation for the show"), areas where people and/or game are kept ("I live on the reservation." "Have you seen the game reserve?"). Lévi-Strauss identifies these reservations with art:

> But, whether one deplores or rejoices in the fact, there are still zones in which savage thought, like savage species, is relatively protected. This is the case of art, to which our civilization accords the status of a national park, with all the advantages and inconveniences attending so artificial a formula. (*The Savage Mind,* p. 219).

Today's artists, especially in theatre, are trying to break out of the reservation. It used to be politics that did it, and it will be again; but now it's consciousness, religion, ritual: the ambition to ''mean something'' and/or to ''change'' people's lives or, at the very least, people's precepts-concepts. Lévi-Strauss also says: ''Art lies half-way between scientific knowledge and mythical or magical thought'' (p. 22). Art specializes in extending what Victor Turner calls the ''liminal,'' the time/space ''in between'' categories, states, rooms. A limen is a threshold, a border: a place you cross over to get from one space to another. Mostly limens are narrow and architecturally negative (a door = a gap in the wall, a place where the wall is not). Limens are passageways through a place where otherwise there's a block or dead-end. In ordinary life people negotiate limens swiftly and easily. Limens look like this:

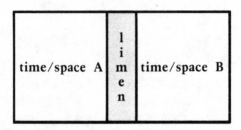

But artists intentionally exaggerate extend blow up elaborate make huge the limen, like this:

The ''work of art'' *is* (in) the limen; and so is the ''work of'' ceremony, ritual, and other operations of human behavior that appear to have no ''good'' (i.e., pragmatic) reason for existing (like religion). I won't elaborate here, or discuss the deep problem: why is art liminal? Those who want to read more read Turner's *The Ritual Process* and *Dramas, Fields, and Metaphors*; and for a psychoanalytic angle, D.W. Winnicott's essays on ''transitional objects and phenomena'' in *Playing and Reality*.

Back to the basic problem. Artists since the Renaissance in the West have been mostly content with *mimesis*: accepting art as a second hand version of a more primary reality. Since the nineteenth century theatre has been the captive of the assembly line: theatre = the production of works (made to be) repeatable on a nightly schedule indefinitely (= as long as there is a market). Performers perform the same actions day in day out; actor training includes techniques to keep the performance ''fresh.'' Such practices are unheard of in cultures where performances happen occasionally, according to need, or through possession, trance, and/or other ecstatic means. In our theatre a hit is a production that imitates the assembly line: each performance is a roughly identical version of the "original product" (= what the critics reviewed/evaluated for potential spectators/buyers). Even avant-garde masters like R. Foreman, Joseph Chaikin, Mabou Mines, etc., etc. participate in this process. The only exceptions I know of occur at the two extremes of scale/size: Robert Wilson designs immense spectacles that extend over time & space and often cost as much as a Broadway production; his works are made for single performances or very short runs. He plays for large audiences, or for free outdoors, and is heavily subsidized. On the opposite end some performers escape the money crunch because their costs are minimal. Stuart Sherman does his one man "spectacles" in theatre lobbies, small spaces, street corners. Like other popular entertainers in whose tradition he is, Sherman is a one-man band, his props are dime-store toys/items. Or take Robert Anton who displays his tiny hand puppets to audiences of no more than fifteen in his own loft. But most theatre artists exist in the middle ground, in the mythos of the middle class: You gotta produce to stay alive.

Now comes a shriek from inside this net; or maybe not a protest but simply a countermove: the introduction into theatre of direct elements of "real" life; or the insistence that theatre *qua* theatre is real life. It's happened in fiction with Truman Capote's *In Cold Blood,* and dozens of autobiographical works, many dressed in the clothes of fiction; and it's happening in film and TV: most remarkably with *King,* an NBC docu-drama that had Paul Winfield and Cicely Tyson playing Martin Luther King and Coretta King, but had Julian Bond play himself, and actual voice-overs of people like Ramsay Clark and Andrew Young; *King* intermingled fiction footage with documentary footage. Some intriguing choices were made: the speech of JFK on TV after the bomb-murder of the four girls in the Birmingham church was done by an actor when footage existed of JFK doing his own talking; ditto for Bull Conners with his (in)famous Birmingham police dogs and fire hoses: though some of that footage—scenes seen from a distance—was documentary. It fell on my consciousness like a mobius loop where you can't tell the inside from the outside: so much of that era is written in TV footage anyway, from the six o'clock news; history has already been edited. But that's not a new problem/situation; it goes all the way back to Thucydides who wrote history the way Aristotle suggested tragedians ought to write drama, selecting not what actually happened but what "ought to have" happened, what "needed to" happen, what—given a certain situation—was logical.

Thucydides: As for the speeches made on each occasion during the [Peloponnesian War], either before or after hostilities had begun, it was difficult both for me, where I had heard them myself, and for my other informants to recall precisely what was said. I therefore recorded what, in my opinion, each speaker needed to say in the particular circumstances, while at the same time I kept as close as possible to the general trend of what was actually said.

Aristotle: The poet's function is to describe, not the thing that has happened, but a kind of thing that might happen, i.e., what is possible as being probable or necessary.

Aristotle goes on to say that the difference between poet and historian is that the first describes the necessary, the second the actual; but as Thucydides says, the historian too is guided by the necessary. Put in plain clothes: we all edit the film of our experience to make sense out of what happens.

Think of the denial of (one kind of) experience that implies, and the arrogance. But also think of the assertion of the power of art(ifice): making words/actions separate from ordinary life, and superior in ability to "get at" or "tell" the truth. Yes, the difference between "experience" and "truth" is editing. Debased editing is mind-fuck brainwash propaganda; illuminated it's truth. Or is the difference merely a matter of "position," of ideology? It leads back to the basic problem again: the mix of real and fictional events, the attention paid to the process of organizing events, the self reflecting on (it)self. In theatre the question is with us: how much "real life" is to be used onstage, and how much self-consciousness is to accompany it (what Brecht called "*verfremdung*" = distance of self from self). In The Performance Group's participatory works—*Dionysus in 69, Government Anarchy, Clothes, Commune* (see my *Environmental Theater*)—spectators were invited, or dragged, into the performance where they became agents of/in the drama: performers themselves to other non or not-yet participating spectators. And it's long been okay for performers to "use" their own lives in constructing roles. Recently these life-elements are not disguised, masked or metaphored as in orthodox acting but enlisted in and as themselves. *A Chorus Line* is constructed from the real lives of the (original) performers, their experiences in theatre, and their private lives. But as replacements occur—*A Chorus Line* is a big Broadway hit, and the show must go on—new performers replace those who originated the roles and former "real life" elements become ordinary traits of fictional characters, acted like any other.

Autodocudrama. Spalding Gray and Elizabeth LeCompte, my colleagues at The Performance Group, have composed *Rumstick Road* (*RR*), a paradigm of a new kind of use of "private" or "natural" events in theatre. *RR* uses techniques of visual theatre—dance, music, abstract movement, forced perspective, various lighting effects (strobe, white-out, back lighting, slide projection)—combined with documentary elements: tape recordings of actual people, slides, direct address to the audience. *RR* shows Gray's relationship to his (suicided) mother, father, grandmothers, and other members of his family. The tapes are interviews Gray made in person and by phone; thus we hear the voices of Gray's father, his grandmothers, the doctor who treated his mother when she was in a mental hospital. The tapes are used in different ways: as sound-track for a lip-synch dialogue between father (played by Ron Vawter) and son (Gray as himself); as telephone call between Gray and his mother's doctor; as illustrated slide lecture narrated by Grandma Gray describing the house on RR and (as she says) "the whole damned family." But these scenes are dialectical: the voices are those of the "real people" but the visuals are those of performers, except for Gray in whose person the two lines of force converge: he is both "real" and "performed," "private" and "public," "natural" and "artificial." Also the body attitudes and movements—the staging of scenes—is according to theatrical logic and not a recreation of the "actual event as it may have happened." In all cases the tapes do not simulate (an earlier) reality but are used as documentary items in a montage that constructs, deconstructs, and reconstructs Gray's consciousness concerning the death of his mother. What the spectator hears is what Gray's family etc. said, but what the spectator sees is the theatric reconstruction shaped by Gray, LeCompte, and the others working on the production. Appalling questions are asked (by implication: by means of imagery): How come Gray's father Rockwell didn't hear the motor of the car running in the garage until it was morning, i.e., until after Gray's mother Elizabeth was dead? Why is the doctor who treated Elizabeth so insensitive when discussing the hereditary nature of schizophrenia?—he pretty well promises Gray the same crisis that overcame his mother. What was the function of Christian Science—its healing techniques, its insistence that the material world doesn't exist—in the death of Elizabeth?

But finally the actuality—the literal density of their presence—of the tapes, slides (Gray found them, he tells the audience, while rummaging through the attic of his father's home), the letters—the rawness of Gray's life—is enprismed in the production itself, including the performers (note: I don't say "actors") whose voices we hear and/or bodies, homes, artifacts we see images of. These members of the Gray family are performers in *RR* though they were never actors in The Performance Group; but we are in a time of deep mixed media: TV especially has trained us to be at ease in the liminal zone between what is happening, or has recently happened, and what is staged; and we are so accustomed to having reality edited, made dramatic (= having high points accented and steady states cut back) that ordinary life is increasingly in need of being jazzed up and simple relaxation is something people have to train long and hard at.

Anyway. For *RR* a conceptual box is built into which the the data is set. This data is not (the traditional) memory-tranformed-into-words-embellished-by-imagination (= fiction) of the writer, but actual fragments of Gray's life-with-his-mother-and-family. This box is not just a container but a bifocal world in receding perspective, and at the bridge of the nose, above but in full view of the audience, Bruce Porter sits controlling tapes and records: the technician as brain as third eye (between the other two). The audience is on what side of this skull? Inside looking out, outside looking in? The audience is seated in a triangle so that the whole space is something like an hour-glass, a single-point vision forced back into bifocality (real life-art life—double world of ordinary life and theatrical reconstruction). In this way the data is mediated into a dance-drama. Gray grows marks around his name until he becomes "Gray": a special version of my colleague presented to/for audiences. Is this any different than what happens in an autobiographical novel, in the diaries of Anaïs Nin, in much poetry? No. But it's startling to have it in the flesh, in the restoration of behavior that is theatre's special task, where the presence of the actor implies, promises, the presence of the "whole" person. What a contradiction! Whole = all, person = mask: and that's what *RR* gives: the wholemask rather than the mask as further cut (up/off) by a plot invented by an author.

One image/action says it: Libby Howes plays Gray's mother. She never speaks—of course not: she's dead when the investigation begins; she's already her own ghost, a compilation of memories and events that thrust themselves into Gray's consciousness very much as a dream (might), as a set of unassimilated actions. Interpretation is for later, in another mind devoted to reintegration. Thus we see Howes shaking her hair to the rhythm of a superloud recording of a Bach partita for unaccompanied violin; her (real) hands holding onto the rain gutter of (the slide projection of) the house on RR; or we watch her and Gray play tag; and we see her examined by Rockwell as she is layed flat out on a table—a rape, a version of parents making love as peeped on by a young boy, a doctor examining a patient or cadaver, a male handling his female merchandise, a theatrical farce: all of the above. But none of these is the image that sticks for me. It's something simpler. Howes is sitting in a chair, a light is shined on her face. Slowly the light is focused: it's a slide of Elizabeth and her children on the lawn, and in front (of the picture projected on the wall) is Howes, her face now a screen onto which the face of Elizabeth is projected in perfect fit. And behind her on the wall a black silhouette where Elizabeth used to be—is, in fact, if only Howes would get up, get out of the way. But Howes doesn't move, no way. The two realities cannot exist in the same space. Elizabeth is absent from the family; Howes is present in the theatre. Then, after a while, the image moves, blurs, Howes rises, but the (Gray) family is gone.

I ask: What is a "wholemask"? It is carrying out a program enunciated over the past 75 years by Gordon Craig, Isadora Duncan, Antonin Artaud, Jerzy Grotowski, etc., etc.: to make art out of the living tissue of the performer, to accept the body of the performer as a signal (a semiotics of flesh):

to make a totally grammatical dance drama in the tradition of the Indian *mudra*. I don't mean a ripoff of Indian (or Japanese or Balinese) style, a gesture language to be read as an alphabet (what Delsartre and Artaud wanted) but an approach that uses affective stuff—words, gestures, pictures, artifacts from "real life"—as moves in a dance: that is, to make out of Elizabeth Gray's suicide—and the reactions of her husband, son, mother, and mother-in-law to it (both before and after that event, an act that bunches time, sucks all diachronism into a dense synchronic drone of automobile motor, Bach partita, father-son dialogue)—a set of sounds/-moves as precise, evocative, and removed from the precipitating situation as an El Greco is from the crucifixion. Sequences of *RR* such as the game of tag, the floating of the red pop-tent when father and son lift a small tent into the air and move it back into an alcove as if it were sucked into another dimension, the family slide show, the talk between father and son before supper, both seated on chairs covered with sheets (= a deserted house, the family having moved away, a ghost scene), the talk between grandmother and grandson, she in a wheelchair played by Vawter disguised with a rubber Woolworth's mask of an old lady: grotesquely true because so many old people seem to end up looking like Woolworth's masks, etc., etc., etc., etc.: *RR* is made of many such images all adapted from everyday behavior, but cleaned up, made exact, tilted a little off-center, and, in rhythmic terms, made into dance. These sequences nudge me away from identification with Gray towards accepting the story as a set of (abstract) moves, as a dance: Brecht's theatre without politics, the distance without the urge to action outside and/or after the theatre. It's the oldest road in Western theatre travelled in the opposite direction from usual. Critics from Aristotle onwards have told us that theatre should be used to approach truth: to find out what is. But Gray and LeCompte, and they're not the only ones, use Gray's life (= truth) as a way of approaching beauty.

It's life for art's sake.

RR operates from the basis that art is primary process. In itself art is redemptive. The performance suggests that the function of living may be to reveal beauty: *RR* was not made to unravel Elizabeth Gray's suicide, or even Spalding Gray's reaction to it; but the suicide and the son's reactions were used to make a beautiful action, a "piece" (= separate peace) as the art-jargon has it. Thus art doesn't imitate life; the flow can flow the other way, as it does certainly in much non-Western theatre, as it does in *RR*.

Street/life, the dis-innocence of children, and systems of transformation. Since Wordsworth at least, children—the concept "child"—have functioned as double agents: they possess or are possessed by prior knowledge, intuition, experience unclouded by cunning; they are demonic, innocent and seductive all at once: from Lewis Carroll to Henry James to Roman Polanski children have exerted an erotic force. Children are to be seen more than ever these days in the avant-garde. And these children are woven into the fabric of their parents' lives. In his review of Squat Theatre's *Pig, Child, Fire!* *New York Times* critic Mel Gussow wrote:

> Squat—short for squatters—is an exiled Hungarian experimental theatre company that began working as a group in Budapest in 1969. [. . .] Banned in Budapest for a performance that was considered by the authorities to be "obscene" and "apt to be misinterpreted from a political point of view" [. . .] Squat certainly deserves that double charge. In one other respect—its involvement of children in questionable parts of the performance—the production is also reprehensible.

Reprehensible? I suppose Gussow refers to one moment when a girl around age eight puts on a pair of lifelike rubber breasts; at about the same time an older woman turns a video camera that had been looking at, and broadcasting to, the audience, against herself, up between her legs into her vagina; or maybe Gussow means the time when the family is at supper, a couple of kids and some adults, eating away while a shoot-out takes place on the street behind them, or when a man dressed in an overcoat and that's all flashes his body, penis and all, at the window.

Using children, it's happening all around this year. *Nayatt School*, the concluding third of the Gray-LeCompte trilogy, has children performing portions of Eliot's *Cocktail Party*, and in other scenes too. I haven't seen *Nayatt* except for rehearsal fragments, so I won't talk about it. But I have seen the last part of the Mabou Mines trilogy *Red Horse, B-Beaver, Shaggy Dog* (all called, punningly, "animations"). *Dog* is four hours long, in three sections, very dense; director Lee Breuer is in the process now of cutting it, but I'm glad I saw it *ur*. The dog of *Dog* is Rose, a female, sometimes a bitch, a wife, a woman in thrall, and she's struggling to find, define, and keep her own consciousness while living a dog's life as the pet companion lover—you name it—of John. The names are transparent, and through them I see Ruth Maleczech, wife of Breuer, and Breuer. Not that *Dog* is an Ibsenite translation of domesticity; far from it: its images are postmodern, dancelike, often abstract, simultaneous scenes, layers of sound coming at you all at once. Much of the technique is directed toward the manipulation of several Bunraku-type puppets. But through all this the obsessive subject, the lens focusing all the material, is the man-woman, husband-wife, master-slave, owner-bought, upperdog-underdog relationship. I can't, won't, describe the imagery—having experienced the piece only once, recognizing in it a masterwork.

But I do want to say that Clover Breuer, eight-year-old daughter of Breuer and Maleczech, plays a main role. Genetically, obviously she is the synthesis—the only possible synthesis—of her parents; and she is herself too. (Isn't that the root mystery of children? how they are and are not what they are made from.) Sometimes Clover is dressed as a grown woman, in shiny gown, parading on high-heels: there's somthing not the-child-at-play in this scene: after all, Clover does it as part of a performance, repetitively, for or at least in front of an audience. Sometimes Clover utters dialogue not made from an eight-year-old head. There's something porny about it (and that's what gets Gussow about Squat), but not in the 42nd Street way. It's this double action-double agent thing artists feel strongly towards kids.

I think Wordsworth, with his Hindu heart and Gita mouth, knows what I'm talking about: Children the most innocent, children the most knowing:

Preserve for thee, by individual right
A young lamb's heart among the full-grown flocks.
vs.
Not in entire forgetfulness
And not in utter darkness
But trailing clouds of glory do we come [. . .]

It's the inverse of the young lamb among the grown flocks that Squat and Mabou play with. Or maybe, more complicated still, the grown-ups project on the purer screens of their own children—for these kids aren't actors picked from open calls—clouded (sexual) strategies the better to see them (and work them through).

However much I want to believe in a child's prior and/or intuitive knowledge I know them to be non-conscious in that thought-out fully bloomed neurotic way labelled normalcy. So the children in these pieces present and re-present a startling naturalness. When Clover is in the bathtub, a tub scaled down to make her appear proportionate to it a full grown woman, dressed in a slinky gown, the soap and water depicted by a fluffy rug (= also shaggy dog fur, also used as the curtain for the whole piece), or when the little girl in Squat eats while the older woman shows the audience her vagina: these children are innocent in their bodies but dressed in (their elder's designed costumes = experience[s]). The naturalness of children is transformed into the artificial of adult analytic imagery. And, yes, I'm turned around by this kind of theatre.

Are they harmed, these children? Should kids work with their parents? So what's different from their ordinary lives, those kids' games we all played on the edges of sexuality? Don't kids who live close to their parents—or in a commune as Squat is—see all these things anyway; and isn't it beneficial to integrate and publicize these experiences? Are these children playing? What are they playing at? Breuer told me he wouldn't let Clover act except with Mabou and with him and her mother close by. After the performance I asked Clover what it was like. "Fun," she said, and smiled. I believe her. And also Clover is "not in entire forgetfulness, and not in utter darkness"—she knows more than her father admits on her behalf she knows and she flirts, plays, and plays at playing. After all, Clover, like the children in Squat, is part of the family: and these plays—*RR, Pig, Dog*—are all family dramas: not in the Ibsenian sense but in a more contemporary context: with our coteries and elites we create a matrix of knowing out of which family dramas emerge just as, in another smallish society, Greek tragedians shaped dramas out of aspects and versions of known myths. It is necessary for community to pre-exist and be larger than the models we make from it if these models (= dramas, performances) are to be "comprehensible," contained in the cupped palms of our consciousness, grasped; and not having a community-in-the-society, we make from our own extended families our groups, the community we need. And what of those who see the work but don't know the families? What of those who see *Oedipus* but don't know the myth?

Squat plays *Pig* in a storefront on 23rd Street not far from the Chelsea Hotel. The audience sits on risers facing a curtain which, when opened, lets them look through the window onto 23rd Street, a fairly busy main avenue of lower Manhattan. The actions onstage—that is, inside the room we paid $4 to gain admission to—are balanced/contrasted by actions in the street; and the actors of Squat are counterpointed by passersby who react to what they see through the window. The playing area is a limen linking two worlds. The setup is like this:

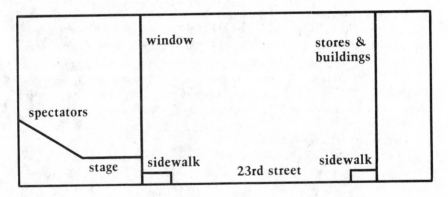

For much of the performance the street is a backdrop offering some gags: passersby doing double takes as they see something bizarre going on behind the window: like a goat eating vegetable scraps as a family sits at table, or a little girl parading around in falsies; and the audience laughs at passersby, like Candid Camera live. (This bit is turned around when the video camera is focused on the audience: spectator after spectator discovers, and reacts, to self on the monitor. It's not merely seeing the self, but knowing the others who comprise an audience are seeing it too: an invasion and immediate publication of privacy.) Often a few knowing persons, having seen *Pig*

from inside, return to watch it from the street. Thus there are three audiences: insiders, outsiders, insiders-who-are-outside. From the perspective of theatre the insiders are natural; from the perspective of street life the outsiders are natural. The insiders-who-are-outside are artificials posing as naturals (to other passersby) or they are double artificials (to insiders). Sometimes the street is used to stage *coups de théâtre* as when a man strolls by, his arm ablaze. I won't discuss the overall flow of actions of the five parts of the performance. These are not significant as drama, narrative, or social commentary. What the actions do is evoke and illuminate the system of transformation from natural to artificial and back. This system is grammatical. Examples of actions by means of which this system can be discerned:

1. A large puppet hangs upside down. From out of its asshole protrudes the head of a man whose face is identical to that of the puppet's; around this man's neck is a noose. For twenty minutes or so this man stares unblinking. The large puppet is removed, the man is hung; then slowly he removes his face (a very cunning mask = both to his "natural" face and the puppet's face); the face underneath the mask is the same. Thus puppet was artificial in reference to the man coming out of its asshole; but the face of the man was artificial in reference to his own face. For a few minutes I was fooled: I thought the unblinking mask was a face. That's because I checked it not against the man's own face (which could not be seen) but against the oversized puppet.

2. A taxicab drives up outside the theatre. A man gets out and draws a gun. Across the street another man stops and draws a gun. Between them traffic flows. Actually a few drivers, seeing the situation, duck as they cruise between the two drawn gunners. Then inside the theatre a woman performer draws a gun and takes aim at the gunman who had arrived by taxi. She shoots, he falls, but the glass between them is not shattered. Again a system is discernible. Taxi = natural = belongs on 23rd Street. Gunmen in the street = ambivalent situation: we in the theatre know this is part of the performance (or at least hope so); those in the street, this is New York remember, take precautions but go on their way. Then the woman drawing a pistol inside certainly makes clear that this is part of the play and that all the gunmen are artificial. The blank shot that drops a person but doesn't shatter glass proves the point.

3. A child is sitting at a table eating. Near her a grown woman is working. To the side a goat is eating garbage scraps. Compared to the adult woman the child is natural; compared to the child actress the goat is natural.

4. A TV camera is aimed at some of the performers. Slowly it pans until it's aimed at the audience. Quickly spectators catch themselves on the monitor. Some mug, some duck, some smile, some appear unconcerned. The camera pans further until it is aimed up the skirt of one of the female performers. The image on the screen is a close up of her vagina. It is a for-

bidden image. Here the natural object of the camera = performers; then an artificial object becomes the subject of the camera; and finally a forbidden part of the body of a permissible subject: a system is established in which we can guess that the next move is to focus on the forbidden body parts of the spectators. Also: the inversion of theatre is made clear: the "natural subjects" of the camera are the "artificial people" = the performers.

5. A little girl performer puts on models of a woman's breasts and parades. She is natural, her falsies are artificial; but were she older her breasts would be mature: she is on the way to becoming what she is now pretending. Outside a spectator does a double take and then calls a friend to peer in also at this bizarre scene. These peeping toms are men—what would my reaction be if they were women? Is it "natural" for men to look at little girls dressed in falsies?

6. At the end of the shoot-out (example two) four police cars scream to a halt in front of the theatre. The performers are checked. They have a permit. But didn't the police know this? Do they arrive every night? Are they part of the script? I ask after the performance: No, they rarely arrive these days, but our permit is running out, they are warning us. To spectators inside, the arrival of the police looks like a TV drama. It's not natural because we know this is a performance. Yet to passersby perhaps scared by drawn guns the arrival of the police is natural, and welcome. To the police themselves it is a little game: Let's get the theatre people tonight!

7. As events slowly unravel inside, a man walking a dog appears at the window. He gazes for a moment, then goes on. A few moments later he reappears; this time his entire left arm is ablaze. He continues to look in as if nothing were happening to him. Passersby do double takes but not one intervenes, no crowd gathers. About twenty minutes later he reappears again: We can see the plastic patches on his coat where the flaming jelly had been applied. He looks inside and then suddenly opens his coat: he is naked. He closes his coat and goes on his way.

What are the oppositions revealed in these examples?

Natural	Artificial
*Street	Theatre
	*Street used as stage, for example for shoot-out, as the place the man with the blazing arm comes from
*Child eating	Woman serving food
Goat eating	*Child eating
Man hanging right side up	Puppet hanging upside down
Man's face	*Mask of man's face
*Mask of man's face	Puppet's face
*Gunmen on street	Woman with gun in theatre

Passersby	*Gunmen on street
*Insiders looking out	*Outsiders looking in
*Outsiders looking in	*Insiders looking out
Performers performing for video camera	Spectators caught by video camera
Spectators watching TV	TV view of performer's vagina
*Child performer	Child performer wearing falsies
Passersby peeping at child	*Child as performer

Etc., etc. The items * = those that figure as both natural and artificial depending on context. This shifting back and forth is mind-blowing. Item after item is established as being either natural or artificial, then is suddenly transformed into the other through the action of the performance. We see the man getting out of the cab: nothing is more "natural" on a New York street than a yellow cab. Then the man draws a gun—this is also natural, though threatening. Then a man across the street draws a gun and I think, Oh, yeah, it's part of the show. This realization is confirmed by seeing the woman inside the theatre draw a gun. It's as if a string connected the man across the street to the man who got out of the cab to the woman inside: the string passes through the window—the precinct of the theatre is extended all the way across 23rd Street.

Ultimately, *Pig* throws into question the "naturalness of nature" and the "artificiality of the artificial." It suggests that whatever the action there is a larger action converting apparent natural to artifical, apparent artificial to natural. It's the dizzying effect that Sartre spoke of decades ago in *Nausea*. It's not easy to say what's been made (by people) and what's "just there." This is true as well of "human nature": the controversy between sociobiologists and their opponents is a dimension of the same question I'm discussing in theatre terms. Is there a natural element at all to human nature? Can we "depend on" our genes (= outside force, natural force, god, etc.) to "tell us" who we are/what to do? What is the justification for the events of this century? How can we get off the hook? Is there a (moral/ethical) hook?

By what grammar are the transformations in *Pig* made? All items and actions are proposed as belonging to an endless series of transformations. These transformations are in the sequence A, B, A, B, A, B . . . nth. That is, there is no end to them. The street = the theatre to those in the theatre looking through the window; but the theatre = the street to those looking through the window in the opposite direction. A child is a social being to the goat, but the child is a natural being to its mother (who is in the process of socializing the child). It's really depressing: perhaps an old nihilistic or dada message. The window between realms of experience opens in (at least) two directions.

I see in *RR, Pig, Nayatt, Dog,* Foreman's work the answer theatre colleagues are giving—maybe not consciously, but still strongly—to the ethical question, the one about the hook of this current century (of atrocities): natural and artificial are transformable/interchangeable quantities. Yes, quantities—like quanta in physics: bundles of relations. And it is natural for theatre artists whose work it is to manipulate behavior across (psychological, cultural, architectural) boundaries to increasingly threaten the peace of mind of those who would like to think . . .

THE
END OF HUMANISM

The
End of Humanism

"Postmodern"? Is it a good term—that is, does it say anything? And if it does say something, is this something what is needed to be said now? First, this isn't just a nominal debate. What a period or style is called certainly influences the kind of work done in, after, and against that style. Think of the words "classical," "modern," "traditional," "romantic," etc. Secondly, an examination of the name may help clarify what kind of theatre is being done these days. But also a word of warning. When there's nothing original the temptation is to take what there is and give it a new name. And when there's no new name around, journalists simply tack "new" onto the generic: thus, "new dance," "new theatre."

The parallel to "postmodern" is "postwar." Postwar means anything that's happened since World War II. And maybe truly this is a proper term, for WWII was the war where the atomic bomb was used and demonstrated the human capacity for extinguishing our own species and for totally ruining the biosphere. It also opened up the post-humanist phase: "ruin" the biosphere for whom? Probably some insect species would flourish in a highly radiated environment. Ruin means made unfit for human life, for other mammals too. Certainly the civilization that followed the introduction of agriculture 8,000 years ago would be finished. So clearly we humans are facing a boundary. No more wars of a total kind—that means no wars that use every weapon available. It means no atomic holocaust.

Along with this goes the disintegration of the power of the nation-states. These story-bearing, culture-bearing units of human history are founded largely on language: France-French, China-Chinese, England-English. But it isn't always that way. The Roman Empire had many people in it who didn't speak Latin; the USSR has many non-Russian speakers in it. Language as the basis for nations and nations as the basis for social, political, economic, and cultural continuity is breaking down. In some places there are too many languages to allow for coherent organization along linguistic lines. This is true of much of Africa, India, USSR; it may be true of Canada, France, Spain, England. More importantly, verbal languages—the bearers of culture, the basis of literature—are being replaced by computer languages. These languages of information bits are universal/elite. Like Sanskrit, computer languages are totally artificial and therefore perfect from the point of view of logic. Being artificial they are understood only by a fraction of the population and spoken only by computers. But these perfect artificial languages are increasingly dominating economic exchange. This exchange is non-ideological in the nation-state sense. The emergence of a universal language controlled by an elite spoken by no one is creating a world order of terrible stability.

Stability? How can I speak of stability with Iran in turmoil, Vietnam occupying Cambodia, Ethiopia and Somalia still at war, Israel and Egypt not at peace, America and the rest of the industrial nations crippled by inflation and faced with recession or depression? And I guarantee that next year will have its own list of "trouble spots." These disturbances are ephemeral and limited. They do not interrupt the exchange of information that is the business of the multinationals; nor will they erupt into a world war defined as an event where total weapons are used and the exchange of information halted.

Stability is measured against a scale of world war and destruction of the biosphere. Against that scale I see the nation-states as already vanished as originators of action. They are retained as entertainment. Crises, wars (of a limited kind), pronouncements of Presidents, Ministers, Generals and the like, comings and going of Shahs, Marshals, Gangs of Four and the like: these are all ways of keeping big populations preoccupied. I define stability as accepting limits to human action—limits that are not the outermost boundaries of knowledge or ability but a frame consciously set around what is "acceptable" defining anything outside that frame as "undo-able."

Accepting such a frame means the end of humanism. I have mixed feelings about that. Humanism measures all enterprise against the scale of what people can imagine and/or do; its motto is, of course, "Man is the measure of all things." Humanism is a very arrogant, anthropocentric, expansionist, and high-energy ideology. Both capitalism and Marxism are humanist. Sociobiology is not humanist. The sociobiologist sees the sources and limits of human action in genetic structures. Sociobiology is but one harbinger among many of the stability I'm talking about. Other harbingers are computer languages, multinational corporations, and postmodern performance. All of these share a rejection of experience—ordinary happenings along a linear plane, a story in the simple sense of "this is what happened,'' or ''once upon a time.'' Instead, these apparently different systems view experience as what the Hindus call *maya* and *lila*—illusion and play—a construction of consciousness. The ''ultimate reality'' lies somewhere else—in the genes say the sociobiologists; in the flow of goods say the economists; in the exchange of information say the multinationals.

What about ''postmodern'' performance? I began by saying that the postmodern is parallel to the postwar. I tried to show that ''postwar'' means something. Postmodern means something too, something close to what postwar means: the organizing of experience in a period when experience is *maya-lila*. Finding ways to organize bits of information so that these bits exist both as experience—what performing art is always dealing with—and as what underlies, is the foundation of, experience. A very difficult job of doubling. Postmodern performance abandons narrative as its foundation. Narrative = experience-as-action. Because experience = *maya-lila*, it is not suitable as action, it is not reliable as action. And because the Western artist—as distinct from the Indian artist—wants the performance not to represent truth but to be truth, or a least truthful, this disintegration of the basis of truth, this destruction of experience, makes for a deep crisis.

The Indian artist solves this crisis by having most of the performance be *lila*—a playing around, with the final moments exploding into another dimension: the sudden eruption of the actual divine during the *arati* ceremony of flame-waving at the end of each night's performance of the Ramlila, for example. At that moment when the camphor flame burns, the crowd strains forward to catch a brief look at the boys-who-are-momentarily-gods. As the flame wanes so does their godhead. At all other times the boys are just ''playing at'' being gods. But even their incandescent moment, seen from the perspective of god-history, is only *lila*. The two spheres of experience converge: at the upper end of the human scale an overlap occurs with the lower end of the divine. What is nearly blinding reality for one is only a game for the other. But we have no such elegant system of interlocking and ascending/descending realities.

Information that since the Renaissance adhered to stories—were drawn into specific patterns the way iron filings arrange themselves according to the ''lines of force'' of a magnet—is now free. The narrative used to be the magnet. Along with the nation-state the narrative has vanished. But the elements of a performance don't just fall anywhere. One of the key assumptions of the postwar/postmodern is that there are no accidents. Everything is connected to everything else; all experience is part of a system. In fact, the unplanned = the terrible, the catastrophic. What used to be thought unplanned or anarchic or chaotic is now organized under the statistical heading ''indeterminate.'' But the works of Cage and others using indeterminacy accounts for only a few of the many postmodern performances, though that few represents postmodern thought in its purest state. Three other main ways of postmodern performance are: organization according to things-space-time (Wilson, Foreman); organization according to self (LeCompte/Gray, Mabou Mines); organization according to the collective (Squat).

Thus the four foundations of the postmodern: 1) indeterminacy; 2) things-space-time or material-chronologic; 3) narcissism; 4) collectivism. These have replaced narrative as the organizing forces of performances. These four "foundations" can be viewed as two groups: 1) the formal: indeterminacy + things-space-time; 2) the human: self + collective.

I think these foundations are linked to "retribalization" which is itself linked to ritual and ritualized performances. The foundations are, after all, techniques. It's ritual that is replacing narrative, and the four foundations are the means of ritualizing performances. So the whole scheme, compared to modernism, looks like this:

	Modern	Postmodern
Techniques:	logic of action	indeterminacy
	stage setting	things-space-time
	character	narcissism
	family &/vs state	collective &/vs tribe
Underlying organizing force:	narrative	ritual
World-view:	nation states	multinational corporations
	competition	collaboration masking as competition
Power:	national leaders who are visible	corporate leaders who are not visible
	politics/economics	economics/religion
Mode:	change	stability
	pragmatism	ideology
	truth is verifiable	maya-lila
Limits:	no limits	framed, limited
Foundation:	in experience, in meaningful actions	in information bits that are behind/below experience
Mood:	active, indicative	passive, subjunctive

This chart links currents in the world with currents in theatre. Few people are making such connections. It's not the old question of "politics" and "theatre" à la Brecht (though that's important too—stage management and education), but the fact that we must find out whether or not history has slipped into a new cycle. Are human societies really entering a new phase, or is it an illusion? An impossible question because if it is a new phase then it will appear to be an illusion; and if there is certainty about entering a new phase that certainty itself is a proof that nothing has changed. I think this is a new time, that a boundary has been crossed. Micro-macro links need to be identified. During this cusp-period theatre is a fine lab and model: one of the places where new customs and their relation to old patterns can be played with, tested, understood.

A few explanatory comments on the chart. When I say that ritual replaces narrative I mean ritual in its ethological sense of repetition, exaggeration (enlarging, diminishing, speeding, slowing, freezing), use of masks and costumes that significantly change the human silhouette. When I say that a postmodern technique is narcissism I don't mean egocentricity. To see "I" at the center of the world is a modern feeling. For the self to see itself and become involved with that reflection or doubling as if it were another is a postmodern experience. To become conscious of this doubling—to posit a third self aware of the mutuality of the other two selves, this geometrically progressive "reflexivity" is postmodern.

When I say that power is shifting from the visible to the invisible, from politics to religion, I don't mean necessarily the religions now familiar to people. I mean the creation of "mysteries" or sanctums, access to which is limited to a special class of people who know the languages of the "truth speakers." These "speakers" may be computers or other artificial beings, and their oracles will slowly organize themselves into a priestly caste. When I say that the mood of the postmodern is passive and subjunctive—and connect this with the idea that the foundation of reality is below and behind experience—I mean that, for example, if a person doesn't feel good she will almost automatically do something to her body to change its programming of experience: a pill, narcotic, massage, whatever. The body is thought of as a processor. Change the endocrine balance, or whatever, and the mood changes. But it's not only the body, and the "I" that is in/of/on the body, but society and the environment that are thought of as manipulable by adjusting its sub-experiential components. Rearranging information is the main way of changing experience.

Now to particular performances. I'll only discuss performances I've seen. I won't try to document performances—I don't know if that can be done, especially with postmodern performances that specialize in sending multiplex signals. Multiplex signals can't be successfully translated into simplex codes, like writing, even when augmented by photographs. This puts theatre in even more jeopardy than before. The art is evanescent. The postmodern is obsessed with information retention. Postmodern theatre is multiplex and therefore unretainable. The only hope is that there will be theatres; then the need for retaining "classical" works will be reduced. Modern theatre had no such problem: narrative usually provided a script in writing and the best commentaries about modern theatre have actually been about drama. Because the written drama carried the narrative, the commentaries were reasonably accurate.

Sending multiplex signals is the main mark of postmodern theatre. Take Mabou Mines' *Shaggy Dog Animation*. (Here I'm depending on my own single attendance in the spring of 1978 supplemented by Ingrid Nyeboe's description in TDR, vol. 22, no. 3, 45-54.) Part I begins with the performers standing in front of a huge radio dial. Most of what they say is filtered through a speaker system. Their voices are intentionally distorted, volumes run up and down. What is spoken is textually represented as a monologue—it is all words of Rose, the dog. But this monologue is broken up among eight people.

> Lines are delivered by one or two voices while words, at times, are repeated by several so that a choral pattern evolves. At times the sound amplification and distortion take over—words and meaning are lost, moods accentuated. Several times the lights as well as the sound control are shut off; an actor turns, faces the audience, flicks a lighter that illuminates his/her face and says a few words in a direct, natural voice. Then, after a split-second blackout, the previous image returns. Related sound effects are interspersed: the sound of water being poured in a dog's bowl, the sound of a whistle, fingersnapping, panting and howling. The literalness of the dog image in the sound is juxtaposed to the ambiguity of language. (Nyeboe, 46.)

The actions of the performers are not illustrating the text. And the text is not telling a story in that direct kind of way customary to the modern theatre. Surely a story can be extrapolated from the actions and words and environment. Rose is a dog belonging to John; Rose loves John; her love is not reciprocated to her satisfaction; finally Rose goes crazy. Rose is a dog a woman a bitch a wife a lover a performer (or two or three) a puppet a concept a way of looking at experience a way of rearranging information to form new experiences a game an artifact. If all you get from *Shaggy Dog* is a hard to understand narrative you've missed the point, and waste [1] effort. There's no way to say in the simplex code of narrative what *Shaggy Dog* presents in the multiplex code of performance. There is no spine to *Shaggy Dog*, no Aristotelian "soul" or "kernel." The intention of *Shaggy Dog* is to deconstruct the experiences of Lee Breuer—author and director—and his colleagues, including his wife Ruth Maleczech and their daughter Clove Galillee, into bits of information and strips of behavior. But what does it all mean? That's another step, a process of reconstruction, that has not yet taken place in most postmodern performances.

Three Places in Rhode Island [PAJ, Fall 1978]—the trilogy developed by

Spalding Gray and Elizabeth LeCompte and other members of The Performance Group (not including me)—stand between the modern and the postmodern. I've watched these three pieces develop over the past four years. I know many of the people from whom the work was made. The way Gray and LeCompte work is for Gray to act out his impulses, to suggest exercises or improvisations. LeCompte "edits" these, makes suggestions for variations, introduces new elements. Other long-time collaborators such as Ron Vawter and Libby Howes also introduce images and actions. There is no attempt at the start of the work to "make a story" or "tell" anything. What the pieces will become depends on what LeCompte sees emerging from all the material presented.

But that's only half of the process. The other half—in the trilogy, not in all postmodern performance—is the use of Gray's life as the main source of the material. His life? Memories of his childhood, his close relationship to his mother whose suicide is the irreducible mystery/unresolvable crime at the heart of the trilogy. The audience doesn't see Margaret Elizabeth Horton Gray except elliptically: as a face in the family slides; as a voice being sung by a performer; as the subject of taped interviews Gray made with his father, his father's mother, a doctor at a hospital where Gray's mother was confined and treated with electric-shock; as someone linked to the fate of Celia Copplestone of Eliot's *The Cocktail Party*; as a female spreading a blanket out on the floor. But it's not Gray's mother who's at the center of the trilogy. Nor is this a memory play where, after a while, the audience gets to "know" the person remembered. The center of the trilogy is Gray's consciousness of his own consciousness of his mother's absence. This consciousness is translated into the multiplex signals of the performance. These signals include the technical: abstract movement, drama, films, slides, tapes, music, lip-synch performing, environmental staging, forced perspective. But it goes beyond the technical into the process of how the trilogy was created: through group improvisation, research, discussion. Yet there is a core: Gray's search through evidence for a sense of who his mother was/is and what happened/is happening to him. She is gone but he remains. He is where the forces of life-history and theatrical reconstruction converge. He stands in front of the audience and introduces himself: he is real and performed, private and public, natural and artificial.

The multiplex signaling of postmodern performance is different from what goes on in modern performing. Of course, the modern and the postmodern coexist. In modern performances lots of signals are emitted: movement, dialogue, setting, music, etc. But this signaling is organized around a clear "line of creation"—such as playwright to director to designers and performers. And the play itself has a "spine" that literally supports and carries all the other signals. The ideal of most modern performances has been to make all the parts of the performance into a unity. Much modern theatre theory deals with the paradox that theatre is "made from" many arts—painting, acting, dancing, architecture—but through the work of the director who "realizes" the intentions of the playwright the performance becomes "itself," a unified artwork. The other modern tendency—typified by Artaud and Grotowski—wants to find the "essential" theatre; what theatre is when stripped of everything not necessary to it: a poor theatre in an empty space. Both these approaches—the unified artwork and the poor theatre—are modern. They are opposed to the postmodern.

There is no need to unify in the postmodern. Unity is inherent in the bits of information that underly experience. Unity may be indeterminate. Signals are sent on many channels simultaneously. Switches from one channel to another are easy. The impulse is transformed—from movement to speech to media to space, etc. Each of the channels can be individually controlled. Artists play with turning up one channel and turning down another. When Wilson slows down movement he is not saying that stasis is essential theatre. He is not "saying" anything: he is doing something. He is playing with the relationship between duration and movement, adjusting the signals in two channels. These channels are separated out from many others. What the extended time and slowed movement in Wilson's work expresses is actually read into the actions by the spectators; or, more accurately, projected onto the actions. A main strategy of postmodern performances is to encourage projections, to serve as screens. And a consequence of individual channel adjustment is that actions previously intuitively generated—actions that "came from" feelings or interactions among performers—are reified, treated "abstractly" or as "formal elements." This reification—and I'm not using the word negatively—though from a humanist perspective it is negative—is one of the things that gives postmodern performance its sense of ritual. It is also a link between postmodern performance and the traditional theatres of Asia. These have had more than an accidental influence on artists like Artaud, Brecht, Grotowski, Cage, Glass, Wilson, Breuer, Brook.

And what is the mudra system of Kathakali except a reification of hand and face gestures? Through a code that is very well developed the performer's hands can say one thing and his face another. Facial decoration is denotative. Sometimes during a performance the performer watches his own hands and reacts to what they are saying, or takes a small mirror attached to his costume and looks at his face and reacts to what he sees. The performer sees the character, and plays with the character. Similarly the layered costume and mask of the Noh actor not only separate him from his everyday life but give him an opportunity to grasp his role not as an extension of himself but as a distinct Other. The hana, or flower, of the mature Noh artist is the performer's ability to play what he is not: it is easy for a young man to play a young woman, but true art for a very old man to play a young woman. Achievement in Noh is tied to the distance spanned between performer and role. This distance is kept intact by strict performance scores, costumes, masks, and various traditions surrounding performances (preparatory rituals, contemplating the costume and mask in a mirror before going onstage, regularized theatre architecture, family traditions, etc.)

Reification doesn't make a performance less moving or deprive it of impact on an audience. Brecht used reification as an anti-emotional device because Western theatre was so loaded in the direction of mimetic naturalism and its accompanying sentimentality. But sentimentality is not tied to any style: Kabuki, for all its stylization, is exquisitely sentimental. But reification does shift focus from the "story being told" to the "way the story is told." Signals are freed from serving the narrative. The key difference between Asian and postmodern theatre is that in Asian theatre channels are controlled by tradition. Tradition—the collective but often not conscious set of conventions or rules—functions the way narrative does in the modern theatre. In Noh even the slightest variation of gesture is considered radically innovative. But at the same time tradition encourages Noh performers to choose one among several costumes for each role—so that performers' moods can be suited to an available range. But this range is also circumscribed according to the season and the occasion of the performance. Postmodern artists are just learning how to play with channels independent of any over-riding principle like narrative or tradition.

I think this situation is temporary because it is volatile. Also because it avoids values: political, personal, cultural programs. Indeterminacy is okay for a perfect world: where in truth every experience is equal to every other. But in a world of conflicting becomings, certain systems, goals, and values are preferred over others. I know that this competition is a source of trouble: who is to fix what is "preferable," and how? As frames of the world-order become more defined the phase of non-traditional art—the non-traditional postmodern—will pass. Rules will be generated to guide the selection and use of channels. I don't think these rules will be narrative. They will come from information processing. A postmodern traditional art is coming.

The link between postmodern performance and ritual is not one of "re-tribalization." Rituals in oral cultures are organized by the memories of elders and shamans, myth, and lore. Performances in oral cultures look like traditional performances. The difference is that traditional performances are organized around both written texts and fixed ways of staging. The written text makes it easier for the traditional performance to "relocate" itself outside of its place and time of origin. Historically this relocation marked the spread of the values attached to the performance: Hinduism and Hindu arts moved together through southeast Asia; Buddhism and Buddhist arts moved from China to Japan. But today there is a great appetite for religious and cultural entertainment detached from value systems, ideologies, and religions.

Noh is not only a ritualized drama but an entertainment for modern audiences, including tourists; it is performed not only in Japan by Japanese but in Kansas by American students. Actually modern transportation is making it possible for oral performances to travel, too. Australian aborigines performed some of their ritual sand drawings and dances on the beach in New London sponsored by the O'Neill Foundation; Sufi dancers have whirled across the stages of Europe and America; Buddhist monks and Shinto priests have played side-by-side with experts of martial arts in a special show developed by the Japanese performer — sidekick of Peter Brook—Yoshi. These are no longer isolated curiosities. Look for more of an amalgamation of traditional and oral performances. International performing is the hope of survival for many forms as the number of pure oral cultures diminishes rapidly to zero. But this kind of performing is actually the use of oral and traditional forms as items in postmodern shows. The multiplex signaling is read cross-culturally; "slots" open in performing art centers' programs: these slots are filled by the "most interesting" and "enriching" material available. It's a kind of P.T. Barnum approach—and an argument can be made that the Barnum circus is a premodern postmodern entertainment.

At the same time traditional and oral performances load into 747s, another kind of oral theatre comes into play in the cities. Evangelical churches, voodoo, healings of various kinds, street entertainers, mimes, magicians, flim-flam gamesters: the theatre of hard times, existing in the margins and creases of society; performances organized around believers transplanted from everywhere to the cities; performances made up to amuse and make a few bucks. These unofficial city theatres are replacing the modern theatre as critics of the social order. What's left of humanism will soon be the slick operator setting up a cardboard box and playing as many deals of three-card monte as he can get in until the cops chase him to the next street corner.

I see four kinds of performances today: oral, traditional, modern, and postmodern.

(see facing page)

Harmonies and contrasts are obvious. What interests me most is the dynamic among these kinds of performance. Before the modern period a regular route (1) was followed as some oral performances became fixed into traditional forms. This is how Noh developed from earlier folk, dance, and religious forms; or how the medieval European cycle plays emerged from Church ritual and popular entertainments. Then, in Europe only, and as an exception to the general way, modern theatre developed (2) out of the traditional. Of course this theatre was part of that great eruption called the Renaissance, and as it worked its way out over more than four centuries this movement became known by a number of names: humanism, positivism, the scientific approach, etc. What seems to be happening now, at

MODERN

Role and performer separate; function of rehearsal to join them.

Originality prized.

Narrative.

Rehearsals used to make details of the performance, but not the text.

Younger performers train outside of rehearsals learning a "grammar" of techniques applicable to any performance.

Artists are individuals who get together for one play at a time; each has his/her career.

Works often critical of the social-political-economic order.

POSTMODERN

Role and performer separate; kept that way in performance.

Originality prized.

Information bits.

No set pattern. Sometimes text is composed during rehearsals.

Training habits vary widely from none to continuous training.

Often organized collectively into groups.

Works mostly non-political, non-ideological.

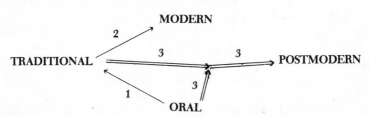

TRADITIONAL

Role and performer separate; separation maintained. Often masks or mask-like makeup used.

Maintenance of score prized. Rules for improvisation.

Little or no rehearsal.

Training in specific roles. Training through imitation or direct manipulation of the body.

Roles are hereditary or in the family.

Artists are part of groups: castes families, etc.

Works often support religious-ideological order.

ORAL

Role and performer separate; often complete identity secured through trance.

No set pattern. Sometimes a strict score, sometimes very loose.

Little or no rehearsal.

Training in specific roles. Or no training at all, merely observation.

Roles are hereditary or in the family.

Artists are part of groups: castes, families, etc.

Works often support religious-ideological order.

least in theatre, is the making of a new route (3). The postmodern is influenced more by oral and traditional ways of making theatre than by modern ways.

There is also a mode not on my chart because I don't know yet how to fit it in. This is the "restored performance"—things like medieval morality plays, nineteenth-century American melodramas, Greek tragedy as it was in Sophocles' times. These exist only for those who study them, either in books or through restorations/re-creations. Restorations are increasing. Maybe this is because films seem to bring us genuine experiences of earlier times in ways more fleshed out and genuine than archaeological or written accounts do. Far from being bereft of performance forms it's hard to lose any these days. The combination of easy travel, appetite for the exotic (we for New Guinea dances, Papuans for rock 'n' roll), and postmodern techniques—and consciousness—of assembling experience out of interchangeable bits results in performances of "this place/time" being put on out of context in "that place/time." Out of every context but the postmodern. For the historical restoration is actually a version of the postmodern. It assumes that spectators, and restorers, can shift temporal channels. Moving through a restored environment involves swift adjustments of frame and accurate processing of multiplex signals.

Thus although I've kept the four categories separate, and haven't even drawn the fifth, there is a collapse of all five into just two. The oral, traditional, and historical are becoming the postmodern; the modern remains separate. The modern proposes the analytic, the critical, the narrative, the skeptical, the contentious—what used to be called the rational, intellectual, and humanist; the postmodern is the religious, the synthetic, the holistic, the ritualized, the uniform. And as I said before, the present phase of the postmodern where messages are sent on separate channels independently—experimentally—is already yielding to a new aesthetic found in Disneyland. Today's kind of multiplexity will resolve itself into the kind of stability found in oral and traditional performances. Stability is descending on the world. I fear it's a necessary stability, a healing of the environment, an acceptance of limits, a *pax atomica*. But as I bid farewell to Faust and Satan I share with them their eternal rage against the end of omnipotence.

107

THE CRASH OF
PERFORMATIVE
CIRCUMSTANCES

A Modernist Discourse on
Postmodernism

The Crash of Performative Circumstances

A Modernist Discourse on Postmodernism

The Mother of Pondicherry, India, was felt by her followers to be immortal. This very old French woman—wife of Sri Aurobindo—was said to be rebuilding her body cell by cell. "Come back in ten years and you will see a young woman." That was in 1972. A few years later The Mother was dead. On the walls of her ashram south of Madras hung exhortations. One of them has stuck with me: "The future of the earth depends on a change of consciousness. The only hope for the future is in a change of man's consciousness and the change is bound to come. But it is left to men to decide if they will collaborate for this change or it will have to be enforced on them by the power of crashing circumstances." I wondered what it meant to "collaborate for this change," and what the "crashing circumstances" might be. To collaborate "for"—if it's not just a grammatical mistake—implies that people must collaborate with each other in order to bring about change. And if they don't, the change will come anyway: some kind of nuclear or ecosystem apocalypse. I thought of Artaud's short definition of his theatre of cruelty: "We are not free. And the sky can still fall on our heads. And the theatre has been created to teach us that first of all." All this seems to be saying that the Age of Humanism is finished. Man is no longer the measure of all things. The cosmos is multicentered, which means it is centered nowhere, or everywhere: everything from holism to narcissism is sanctioned.

At The Mother's ashram I lay my head on that old lady's knee, as was the custom in having *darshan* (literally, a vision) of her. Upon leaving her I wrote in my notebook: "She looked at me. I left trembling. I am confused, unknowing. Her look penetrated. She did not know, she saw." Saw what?

I ask now ten years later. My notes from that day continue: "Doubts—fundamental denials, remain, but something has happened, is happening." And I hear now an old Buffalo Springfield lyric: "Something's happening here/ what it is ain't exactly clear."

Yes. We've been told by our visionaries, our demographers, our artists and our ideologues. Change is upon us.

Our Mothers, Malthuses, Artauds, and Marxes agree on that. Our only liberty in the matter is whether we shall collaborate in effecting this change or be its passive victims/beneficiaries.

Beneficiaries of nuclear holocaust? Of ecological catastrophe?

And will the change be from consciousness or from circumstances?

And what kind of change are these dreamers dreaming of? Does anyone believe in the stateless society of Marx? Or any other paradise?

The Mother tried to demonstrate in her own body how consciousness can triumph over circumstances. She failed. Is her failure definitive?

Marx, the perfect modernist, saw history as man-made, and within our control. Brecht tried to push this idea of humanist responsibility in his plays. But Brecht couldn't even control Mother Courage: she turned tragic right on the Berliner Ensemble stage. And our species collectively—as communities, nations, or associations of nations—has not succeeded in reconstructing human history any more than The Mother succeeded in reconstructing her own single body.

This kind of thing is giving the future a bad smell.

I am a person = a mask, a multiplicity, a process to sound through. I live on and in the limen separating and joining the modern from and to the postmodern. All those linked prepositions seem necessary. Pre/positions: the places I'm in before I'm in place—places that are not simply defined but lead in at least two directions. The attention given by so many to Zen and its insistence on "present consciousness," the center, the now, is partly explained by the terrible drag of both past and future. What I mean by "modern" and "postmodern" I've tried to explain in another writing, "The End of Humanism." But I'll add some more here.

My furious obsession with writing—I've filled sixty-five notebooks with more than 20,000 pages over the past twenty-six years—is a modern obsession with "getting it all down," of catching the flopping fish of experience. Yet my very existence as a "theatre person" who "makes plays"—experiences that can't be kept, that disappear with each performance, not with each production but with each repetition of the actions I so carefully plan with my colleagues; each repetition that is never an exact duplication no matter how closely scored, how frozen by disciplined rehearsals—this very existence in/as theatre is postmodern. For the theatre is a paradigm of "restored behavior"—behavior twice behaved, behavior never-for-the-first-time—ritualized gestures. And if experience is always in flow, theatre attempts, in Conrad's words, to wrest "from the remorseless rush of time" precise moments of experience. And the domain of theatre is not, as Stanislavski thought, psychology, but behavior. Writing, of course, also tries to immobilize experience—but writing translates experience into this system of graphemes you are now reading. And film, a trickster, is another system of writing: a behavior agreeably locked into a mechanical process where it can be edited on a table. Only theatre—live performance, from dance to circus to rituals to plays to sports—works directly with living persons. In theatre the flux and decay of ongoing living is asked to halt, become conscious of itself, and repeat. A paradox Heraclitus already knew about, and so did the author(s) of the Sanskrit treatise on performance, *Natyasastra.*

The postmodern is possibly a liminal bridge in history, a period conscious of itself, its past, and its multiple potentials as future. By postmodern I mean:

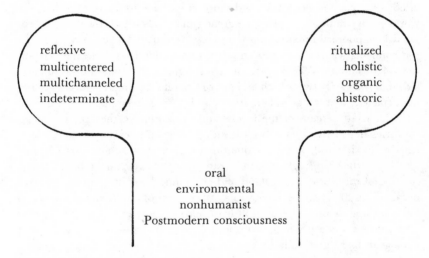

reflexive
multicentered
multichanneled
indeterminate

ritualized
holistic
organic
ahistoric

oral
environmental
nonhumanist
Postmodern consciousness

These tendencies are not "resolvable" into a noncontradictory whole. Postmodern holism more than tolerates contradictions. In some of its tendencies we have the hilarious and scary monologues of Spalding Gray and the incredibly energetic performative outflowing of Jeff Weiss, both superbly narcissistic, truly looking deeply into the waters and seeing only themselves worthy of the fullest love. In other manifestations the postmodern births collective works like Mabou Mines' *Dead End Kids* whose range extends from Faustus to J. Robert Oppenheimer, from alchemy to nuclear apocalypse. The postmodern includes both environmentalists helping people gain the consciousness of global ecosystems necessary for survival and one logical outflow of that consciousness in action, an Orwellian world of total information/action control.

Why, you ask, must knowledge of systems lead to tyranny? *Scientia est potentia* is an old saying, still true.

Or to put it another way: Why, I ask, must knowledge of systems lead to paradise?

I keep a file of clippings called "Doomsday." It's my common book of despair.

Some of the titles: "Causes of Cancer Called Numerous," "32 Nations Close to Starvation," "Toxic Trace Elements: Preferential Concentration in Respirable Particles," "House Report Fears World Starvation," "Help is Urged for 36,000 Homeless in [New York] City's Streets," "Stratospheric Pollution: Multiple Threats to Earth's Ozone."

The gloomiest of all is the *Global 2000 Report* issued by the Carter Administration in July 1980 and summarized in *Science* (1 August 1980): "If present trends continue, the world in 2000 will be more crowded, more polluted, less stable ecologically, and more vulnerable to disruption than the world we live in now. . . . Despite greater material output, the world's people will be poorer in many ways than they are today." The *Global 2000 Report* confirms what we already know, but infrequently stare in the eyeball: that $450 billion a year is spent on arms, against $20 billion on economic aid; that the gap between rich and poor is increasing; that resources are being depleted; that the global environment is losing life-support capabilities. "By 2000, 40 percent of the forests still remaining in the less developed countries in 1978 will have been razed. The atmospheric concentration of carbon dioxide will be nearly one-third higher than preindustrial levels. . . . Desertification (including salinization) may have claimed a significant fraction of the world's rangeland and cropland. Over little more than two decades, 15-20 percent of the earth's total species of plants and animals will have become extinct—a lost of at least 500,000 species."

If true, this is a prediction of more than genocide—but of some mean neologism like "globacide."

Yet the ecology movement can't get many people out into the streets. The disarmament movement is just getting off the ground in the U.S.A.

Is it that people don't believe the predictions? That doomsday is too gross to be incorporated into consciousness? That people, fearful, are trying to take care of Number One, letting the rest go rot?

All of the above.

Already in *Tristes Tropiques,* published in 1955, Claude Lévi-Strauss saw what still only a few, relatively speaking, accept:

Now that the Polynesian islands have been smothered in concrete and turned into aircraft carriers solidly anchored in the southern seas, when the whole of Asia is beginning to look like a dingy suburb, when shanty-towns are spreading across Africa, when civil and military aircraft blight the primeval innocence of the American or Melanesian forests even before destroying their virginity, what else can the so-called escapism of travelling do than confront us with the more unfortunate aspects of our history? Our great Western civilization, which has created the marvels we now enjoy, has only succeeded in producing them at the cost of corresponding ills. The order and harmony of the Western world, its most famous achievement, and a laboratory in which structures of a complexity as yet unknown are being fashioned, demand the elimination of a prodigious mass of noxious by-products which now contaminate the globe. The first thing we see as we travel round the world is our own filth, thrown into the face of mankind. [New York: Atheneum, 1974, p. 38]

Travel around the world? Try any New York street. And yet the rage to clean it all up has fascist harmonies: Mussolini making the trains run on time; Reagan eliminating social programs and preaching that everyone must sacrifice: as if asking the executive to do with only two cars is equivalent to asking the unemployed to do with only two meals.

Lévi-Strauss's India is not that of Baba Ram Dass, or any of the others who have returned to America saffroned with holiness. No, the French anthropologist looks with earlier, modern, rational eyes, and feels with a heart pumping material blood as he describes conditions in Calcutta:

> . . . at Narryanganj, the jute workers earn their living inside a gigantic spider's web formed by whitish fibres hanging from the walls and floating in the air. They then go home to the "coolie lines," brick troughs with neither light nor flooring, and each occupied by six or eight individuals; they are arranged in rows of little streets with surface drains running down the middle, which are flooded thrice daily to clear away the dirt. Social progress is now tending to replace this kind of dwelling by "workers quarters," prisons in which two or three workers share a cell three metres by four. There are walls all around, and the entrance gates are guarded by armed policemen. The communal kitchens and eating-quarters are bare cement rooms, which can be swilled out and where each individual lights his fire and squats on the ground to eat in the dark.
>
> Once, during my first teaching post in the Landes area, I had visited poultry yards specially adapted for the cramming of geese: each bird was confined to a narrow box and reduced to the status of a mere digestive tube. In this Indian setting, the situation was the same, apart from two differences: instead of geese, it was men and women I was looking at, and instead of being fattened up, they were, if anything, being slimmed down. But in both instances, the breeder only allowed his charges one form of activity, which was desirable in the case of the geese, and inevitable in the case of the Indians. The dark and airless cubicles were suited neither for rest, leisure nor love. They were mere points of connection with the communal sewer, and they corresponded to a conception of hu-

man life as being reducible to the pure exercise of the excretory functions. . . .

. . . Nowhere, perhaps, except in concentration camps, have human beings been so completely identified with butcher's meat. [ibid., pp. 128-9]

Nowhere? Try the toilets at Penn Station, Manhattan, two blocks from where I live and write this. Here's a little description from the Sunday *New York Times,* 8 March 1981, describing the nightly rituals of some homeless "bag ladies":

At 11 p.m. the attendant goes off duty and women rise from separate niches and head for the bathroom. There they disrobe and wash their clothes and bodies. Depending on the length of the line at the hand dryers, they wait to dry their clothes, put them in their bags or wear them wet. One woman cleans and wraps her ulcerated legs with paper towels every night.

The most assertive claim toilet cubicles, line them with newspapers for privacy and warmth and sleep curled around the basin. Once they are taken, the rest sleep along the walls, one on a box directly beneath the hand dryer which she pushed for warm air. One of the women regularly cleans the floors, sinks and toilets so that no traces of their uncustomary use remain.

Maybe you're thinking poverty has always been with us—Dickens described scenes that, subtracting their sentimentality, were every bit as dehumanizing and brutish. I look at this same *New York Times* issue and find numerous advertisements on page two for diamonds. In fact, newspapers—like TV—are our best evidence of the gap between the experience of the poor, the rich, and the middle classes. The stories focus on what it's like to be poor—to suffer urban life with its violence, filth, insensitivity—while the ads abound with luxury items: furs, perfumes, lingerie, cars, vacations; or with remedies that drug the middle class: sleeping pills, nasal sprays, stomach soothers, bowel movers.

I know I'm "oversimplifying," but I need to do it. Why? Because a good part of my daily life is spent attempting to negotiate among these "simple" experiential contradictions.

Not yet have I found the way to include—not negotiate around—these contradictions in my work, in my theatre, my writings, my teaching.

None of the political menus—the Marxists, the capitalists, the democratic socialists, the terrorists, the dropout communalists—is right for me. That is, I don't believe in their programs, promises, outlooks. And I don't like the people who run their organizations. Ditto for the religious solutions and the solutions of "consciousness," wherein I get my act together, and you get yours, and yours, and yours . . . until history turns around. I don't buy that approach either.

Frederick Turner, co-editor of the *Kenyon Review,* a poet and author of the science fiction novel about the theatricalized future, *A Double Shadow* (New York: Berkeley Publishing Corporation, 1978), has communicated to me, in a letter, a more hopeful future:

> We are capable of accurate prophecy, subject only to the co-prophecy of other minds and other organized realities; and that prophecy is the same as action. To put it all more simply, it's up to us which alternative will come about. There is no such thing as the future yet and this realization makes us public men, and forces a kind of civic piety upon us. Because if things do go wrong, we are to blame. The plea of powerlessness is no excuse: the power of others is created by our own opinions of it, and nothing more. We can change our opinion, and we do it by making one alternative more beautiful than another.
>
> If we destroy ourselves in a nuclear holocaust or eco-catastrophe, it won't be because of some kind of technological determinism, or innate drive or conspiracy of the powerful or economic forces of history; it will be because we chose to, collectively, and we chose to because we considered that future to be the most beautiful, and we considered it to be the most beautiful because we imaginatively constructed it to be so. Art has the exalted function, the world-saving function, of imaginatively constructing other futures which do not involve the *gotterdammerung* of mass suicide. I don't mean namby-pamby assertions of moral principle or nonviolence. They only increase the desirability of what is forbidden (Blake). Most ecology freaks are imaginatively mass-murderers. They would like to cleanse the filthy, desirous, complicated, upsetting, demanding, loving vermin of humanity from the face of the earth. They're the obverse of the Strangeloves, and less attractive because less straightforward.
>
> The appeal of nuclear holocaust is that it upstages history. Without the expense of imaginative effort it instantly makes our generation more important than Homer's, or Christ's, or Shakespeare's. It's the ultimate oedipal put-down, the final punk concert. If you want my opinion about what I think will happen if we (I mean the artists and imaginative creators in all the fields) do nothing, then I think we will destroy ourselves because we dearly, pruriently want to. It's such a cheap rush.
>
> Feeling is so hard to construct that instead of doing the work of construction we've spent a couple of centuries cracking out the feelings stored in the old sociocultural structures like oilmen pumping steam into old domes to get out the last trickles. . . . We've not much left, we fear. Our image of the universe has been of entropic systems that radiate crude energy by destroying themselves and others. The nuclear holocaust is a perfect picture of our self-excusing version of the universe. If the universe is running down, if there's only so much energy and value to go around, let's use it all up in one go, go out with a bang not a whim-

per. Better that than have to invent, think, love, work, take risks. Nuclear holocaust is dead safe. You know exactly where you are with it. It's a future with no variables: the Marxist/Capitalist ideal.

Of course the universe isn't running down, if we realize that it's made of information not of energy. Energy is simply information divided by an unreal measure, space. The world is growing and learning to speak, like a baby, and its information is increasing all the time. We are the chief agents of that increase; in terms of information rather than space, we are the biggest objects in the universe and the galaxies are little specks upon our skins. But the risk is, we could choose to deny our opportunity.

So it's up to us. I predict that we will create subjunctive worlds, not the death-bang. The fact that that prediction is a resolve, an intention, doesn't make it any less of a prediction, but more of one. The road to heaven is paved with good intentions.

Yes, it's the old Protestant Ethic standing on its head. But Turner understands The Mother's "change of consciousness," and Arthur Clarke's *Childhood's End* too. Turner comprehends that the postmodern epoch is one of information. But, as anthropologist Ray Rappaport reminded me, information and meaning are not the same. An abundance of information uncomprehended, or transformed into ritual formulae, is not meant, but either ignored or felt.

An excess of uncomprehended information over the past 200 years has bred a prodigious science without a comparatively robust religion—or morality, if you will. So here we are, armed to our nuclei, and just about permitted to throw radioactive pies in each other's faces. For farce is what it is: an excess of violence that no one really believes is real. But wait till it explodes. But is Turner right in prescribing "subjunctive worlds"—a heavy dose of theatre? Is our moral balance to be found among the clowns and acrobats?

Before taking up that one, a caveat about the "cheap rush" of nuclear holocaust. It won't be so cheap. It won't be a big death bang but a series of painful whimpers. There are films of Hiroshima and Nagasaki—and a little booklet, printed in Japan, entitled *Give Me Water—Testimonies of Hiroshima and Nagasaki*:

What I saw under the bridge was shocking: Hundreds of people were squirming in the stream. I couldn't tell if they were men or women. They looked all alike. Their faces were swollen and gray, their hair was standing up. Holding their hands high, groaning, people were rushing to the river. I felt the same because the pain was all over the body. . . . I was about to jump into the river only to remember that I could not swim.

When I was about to get to our home, a middle-school student in our neighborhood told me that my son Shiro had been spared. It was almost unbelievable. . . . I examined him and found that his left hand from the elbow to the finger and upper half of his head above his nose were burnt. I too felt that he would be all right soon. I thanked her and carried him on my back to the hospital. . . . My son was only given ointment for his burns. And he started a high fever in the morning of August 9. . . . At about 4 in the afternoon, Shiro threw up some stuff which was as dark as coffee several times and passed away in two minutes.

Then I realized for the first time how my mother looked. She had been hit by the blast as she was picking eggplants to feed us at lunch. She was almost naked. Her coat and trousers were burnt and torn to pieces. Her hair had turned to reddish-brown, and was shrunken and torn as if she had had too strong a permanent. She got burnt all over the body. Her skin was red and greasy. The skin of her right shoulder, the portion which bore and lifted the beam, was gone, revealing bare flesh, and scarlet blood which was constantly oozing out. Mother fell exhausted on the ground. . . . Mother began to feel pain. After groaning and struggling, she passed away that night.

On the day of August 6 . . . I was 3 months pregnant. Since I was carrying a baby, my chore was to take care of lunch some distance away from where the bomb hit. That's why I was spared. . . . A week later the often-mentioned atomic disease hit me. All my hair was gone, and I had a rash all over my body. My teeth were shaken up as bloody pus kept coming out from the gums. Because of vomiting blood and bloody excrement I felt so weak that I almost gave up. . . . I may have been lucky. I survived and made a steady recovery. I delivered Yuriko on February 24 next year without much trouble. She was small indeed and the midwife told me, "You really have to take care of this baby." . . . She was brought up mostly on milk. When her first birthday came, she could not say a word. At the second birthday it was the same except that she could barely manage to crawl. When she was four or five years old I tried hard to teach her to walk and she started walking, but she was lame. . . . She came to school age. But I thought she could not keep up even in kindergarten. . . . We kept our hope every year to no avail. The sixth year came and Yuriko was exempted from schooling. Around that time doctors of the Hiroshima University Medical School came to survey the survivors in the Ohtake area. They examined her and took her picture. She was found to have the small-head syndrome cause by the atomic bombing. Up until recently I thought Yuriko was the only example. . . . Having had no pleasure in her life, she became very fond of movies. . . . She must look strange—standing lame, muttering something to herself in front of a movie poster. People look back at her from curiosity. School-children play lame before her or try to drive her away as if she were a dog. Yuriko herself seems embarrassed to be stared at or have somebody around. Nowadays she tends to stay all day at home and spends the time with TV and radio. That makes her physically weak; she gets easily tired even by just taking a short walk. . . . She is so occupied with movies, TV, and radio all day, from morning till she goes to bed, that she can't make it to the bathroom on time. . . . I have a grandchild who is 3 years old. I think Yuriko is a little bit more immature than him. She is now 20 years old.

Well, there are as many testimonies as casualties, multiplied by the number of people who knew persons who were there. Millions. Thus the inheritance of the twentieth century: the concentration camps of Europe, the atomic bombs of Asia. "Of" Asia? No, in Asia, but of Euro-America. So, though Turner almost convinces me with his optimism, these daymares return. For the horrors of war are not nighttime things but the outcomes of our most scrupulously rational thinkings, of our most highly exercised cerebral cortexes. More nightmares might be among the remedies recommended for the generals, the Haigs, Weinbergers, and Reagans. I don't exempt the warriors of other nations; I just don't know their names.

The final scene of *Dead End Kids*—the Mabou Mines performance piece that's all about nuclear energy, experimentation, and holocaust—is a parody of a sleazy nightclub act. The comic invites a young woman (a plant) from the audience onto the stage. He makes sex jokes with/against her. He uses as a prop a dead plucked chicken—the kind you get at the supermarket. This prop is naked flesh, dead yet vulnerable, not being used to feed anyone but to stand for the penis, the vagina, the insides of the body, the victims of atomic bombs, the raw meat we are when we are nothing else. And have you ever noticed how chicken skin is the color of some Asians? The audience reacts strongly to this scene. Some offended, some amused, some sickened. This scene—which people advised director JoAnn Akalaitis to drop—is a scary commentary on the current level of consciousness not only about things nuclear but the whole drift of our species toward globacide.

Having lost a sense of the sacred, we also lose awareness of the terrible. So what's so bad about atomic warfare, lead in the air, ozone depletion, extermination of nonhuman species? Everything can be talked about, understood, dealt with, defended against.

I'm not talking about the technological imperative: our almost automatic belief that for every problem there's a solution.

I'm talking about something happening to language, including the languages of art. To "look something in the face"—to end taboos, to be able to discuss it openly—is believed somehow to be equivalent to solving the problem. Or at least rendering it less dangerous. But really this openness is a way of deadening.

Again it's an invasion of the rational into spheres of nonrational—what word can I use? certainly not thought—process. The deep process of imagination has been contaminated.

Now back to Turner's future of subjunctive worlds, which is a call to reimagine. Can it be done as efficiently as scarred landscape is reforested, or depleted fisheries farmed? Are we arriving at the paradox in human self-directed evolution when the unconscious, the primary process, is to be directly fertilized? Having spent so much energy in training the cortex to control the rest of the brain, are we now to seek out a limbic resurgence?

There's no way back to a genuine premodernism. Who wants it anyway? Human life then was threatened by the environment. Today human life threatens the environment. What we need is a balance.

In the sixteenth century, after some bloody battles using rifles and cannons, the shogunate in Japan decided that this method of warfare was costing too much. Too many lives were being lost, brute firepower was replacing the elegant earlier ways of warring. So firearms were banned, and for nearly 300 years Japan continued its former traditional ways of doing battle.

In today's Papua New Guinea, warriors arrive by motorbike at the battle grounds. They park their vehicles and fight with bows, arrows, and spears. They know about guns, but know too that their small populations would soon be decimated if guns were used.

Peace loving? No. But there are limits to war. These are very low. War, if not abolished, needs to be made a handcraft again.

How can performance assist in this? And in the other transformations necessary for human social survival.

If you're waiting for an answer that will reveal to you the meaning of life, go on to the next essay.

Experimental theatre in America—and in Europe, too, from what I can gather—is in a bad way. Experiment means, literally, to "go beyond the boundaries." There's not much of that going on these days. As things have gotten desperate outside of theatre, they've become more conservative within it. The great period of experimentation that began in the fifties ended by the mid-seventies. In my essay "Decline and Fall of the (American) Avant-garde" I discuss the history of this period and the reasons for the decline in detail. No need to belabor the story here. What I want to focus on is the phoenix aspect: what's rising from the ashes. For the experimental period has given us a foundation in practice for what Turner calls for in his letter.

This foundation is a performance art based on postmodern consciousness. A consciousness that relies on bundles and networks, on spheres, modes, and relations. It is a performance world reminiscent of medieval totalism, where actions are instantly transformed into relations. This performance world is the source of renewals of religion—and by religion I don't mean only the known creeds, most of which are frozen, nor do I mean theology. I mean sacralizing the relations among people: creating special, sacred, nonordinary—you pick your descriptive adjective—space and time. And enacting within, or in relation to, such space/time events that resonate significance not only to the audience but also to the performers.

Ironically, the modern period, which made "man the measure of all things," proposed an idea that could not yet operate openly. Forget for now whether this program was projecting a social order dominated by males at the expense of females, and whether there is enough innate difference in aggressive potential to make the male-female argument worthwhile at the level of "who rules." The modernist program was humanist—extraordinarily noble and optimistic. But it didn't work out so well for whales, forests, and billions of human beings born outside of Europe, North America, Japan, and a few other domiciles of superiority, economically/militarily speaking.

Maybe, if you like Turner's scheme of reality, the humanist world was a subjunctive posibility dreamt in the fifteenth century a few epochs before its time.

The posthumanist, postmodern subjunctivity we are in the first moments of dreaming these days may be better suited to our capabilities. I see ten qualities of this postmodern subjunctively projected future.

1. It is multicentric. Everything, or nothing, is at the center. Experiences exist without frames, giving time/space a sense of "insideness," of being-in-it. Experience—flow alternating with reflexivity, an awareness of flow even while not stopping flow—replaces analysis. This multicentricity demands the construction of holistic, global systems. Because there is no center there must instead be an order of relations, not a hierarchy or a pyramid or a circle with a center point, but more like what the earth's atmosphere looks like from close space: whorls, and constantly shifting but totally interrelated patterns of movements. Socially, such comprehension of a global eco-system leads to a feeling of limitedness, of feedback, recycling, inner-focusing. It's not too big a leap from there to ideas of reincarnation, which is a way of saying there is feedback of personal-being-soul-stuff as well as of the more obvious material stuff.

But.

Actually, the concept of multicentricity and holism do not contradict but need each other. Both indicate fully significant worlds, and both indicate the dominance of rhythmicity over all other kinds of space/time orderings. Not lines, which mean single-point perspective, but rhythmical relations, which mean dance.

This danced universe is opposed to the modernist ideal of an ever-expanding—that is, receding—point of origin or frame of reality, and an equally expanding human consciousness that regularly "breaks through," leading to "new fields" that sooner or later are "known." Clearly, that world is the one from the age of great discoveries by Euro-American navigators and astronomers, the line from da Gama and Galileo to Glenn and *Voyager*.

This line need not end for multicentricity to take over. Multicentricity is just that, multiple.

2. The ability to support, even delight in, contradictory or radically paradoxical propositions simulataneously. From the sound of one hand clapping to a frameless yet limited cosmos. Here's where clowns and shamans come in. And theatricalism as the realm of reality founded on projecting experiences that are true/not-true.

3. The process of knowing that the "thing" is part of the "thing and the experiencer of the thing." All observations are participations. And all participations are creations. The modern ideal:

becomes the postmodern:

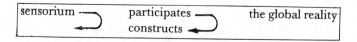

Also reflexivity develops as each global reality is experienced both from within and from without simultaneously. The experiencer is also that which experiences herself experiencing. Dizzying, fun, subjunctive (as if, would, could, should); terrifying, hard to hold onto, uncertain, relative.

4. In the modern period people could correctly speak of absolutes. In the postmodern each set of relationships generates transformations that hold true for this or that operation. As modern seeing becomes postmodern experiencing, postmodern performance leaves the proscenium theatre and takes place in a multiplicity of spaces. The proscenium theatre is known for two qualities: there is a best seat in the house; there are clearly defined areas for different activities—stage, backstage, house, lobby. Half the structure belongs to the performers, half to the spectators. The postmodern performance space is strictly relational: you don't know what it is until you use it for whatever you are doing. Although it seems that now we're in a reactionary period where the proscenium theatre appears to be making a comeback, this is only an illusion. Of course orthodox spaces are being used, but so are countless new spaces that twenty-five years ago weren't. Like galleries, lofts, clubs, courtyards, beaches, roofs, streets. The environmental possibilities of performance have expanded to include dozens of new territories.

Not only space, but time too. I mean time as a when and time as an experience of. Again this emergence of rhythmicity.

5. The use of multiple channels of communication. This goes beyond the human. Everything from genetic codes to lasers to body language to pulsars seems to be "saying" something. An aspect of the totality of significance. And in performance it is no longer necessary to rely on the linguistic channel as the dominant one. There is multicentricity of communication as well as of experience and cosmic construction.

This is the operational feature of Turner's subjunctive worlds. As many worlds as can be imagined can be communicated. Or maybe it's more interesting the other way: as many worlds as can be communicated can be imagined.

The artistic mind—the mind that specializes in inventing possible worlds—is emergently important.

How does this jibe with Lévi-Strauss's painful witnessing of humans reduced to meat and excretion? The horrors he writes of are the products of humanism. The delights of the connoisseur and the luxuries of the rich are resting on the backs of the poor. These horrors will not just go away. But I doubt whether revolution as conceived of from the eighteenth through the twentieth centuries is the answer either.

How to eliminate or at least reduce these horrors is the main thing this writing is playing with.

Playfulness may be part of the answer.

6. The alternation of flow and reflexivity. Sometimes we're in it, sometimes we're out of it. Even when we're out of it, we're in it; and even when we're in it, we're out of it watching ourselves in it.

A very theatrical way of doing things. Rehearsing, stopping, repeating, taking the action up in the middle, playing around with it, making it "better."

Also a way of theatre-going, wherein spectators do not agree to disbelieve in what's going on. This disagreement to disbelieve preserves individual experience in a collective act.

The alternation of flow and reflexivity leads to fragmentation as well as holism.

The postmodern transmutation is not of gold but of experiences, not to perfect heavy metals but to offer new ways of being, which are ways of doing, ways of performing.

7. Dreams are not considered only secondary reflections of hidden primary processes. Dreams are not automatically in need of interpretations that strip them of their imagery.

In 1977 I ran a dream workshop at American University. During two hot weeks about a dozen of us shared sleeping space and performance workshop space. We observed each other sleep and dream, and experimented with controlling our dreams and performing dreams immediately upon being awakened from them. Systematically some of the differences between waking and dreaming consciousness were elided. Persons experienced mutual dreaming (where two or more dream the same dreams, or elements of the same dream) and lucid dreaming (a dream where you know you are dreaming—an ultimate in reflexivity). Finally we staged for ourselves a sequence of dreams, and acted out within the Washington area aspects of our dream-lives.

The workshop was scary. But I'd like to resume its experiments.

Also to look more to dreams as Aborigines experience them. As gateways to the first time, as a way of making present that first time.

Interestingly, dreams in several cultures are the sources of dances. Dreamers learn dances while dreaming, and bring the dances back.

Dreams, vision quests, trance.

The nightlife of the brain. What worlds are there waiting to be staged.

But not dreams in their mystical sense. Dreams, rather, as a continuation and elaboration of day-brain activities. In other words, along with the expansion of brain activity to include both noncortical and cortical languages—body languages as well as verbal languages—a parallel integration of the night brain and the day brain. This has been going on a long time. The theories of Freud are based largely on his investigations of dreams. But he attempted to interpret dreams rationally, to see them as texts presented by the unconscious to be sorted out, understood, by the conscious. Such interpretation needed the assistance of another, the analyst. So that, in fact, there were three or four interactants in Freud's scheme: the conscious and unconscious of dreamer and analyst. I don't want to abandon Freud's process, but add to it the ability to apprehend the dreaming directly, without translating it or reducing it.

To a degree, this is what Robert Wilson and Richard Foreman have been doing. Wilson in regard to time, the showing in space of different rhythms of time, different ways of thinking-doing, including the ways of dreaming. And Foreman by his insistence on trying to represent in the theatre as clearly as possible the primary process of his own thinking un-edited. And, as it is becoming increasingly clear, some day thinking is like night thinking, if we let it come through unedited. Writers have known this, but it is taking longer to get through to the theatre. Cultures other than Euro-American have also known, and practice, performances based directly on primary process activity.

8. This relates to accepting body thought alongside cerebral cortex thinking. As the concept of body thought is unpacked, people will discover how many different modes of thought our species can do. We already know that learning and artistic expression can occur autonomously, like dreaming. Again dance is a good model, for much dance learning is at the neuro-muscular and subcortical brainstem levels. The development of body thinking is not threatening to cortical thinking, anymore than the discovery of left-brain, right-brain tendencies threatens word language. What I'm arguing for is the coexistence of many different kinds of thought, and a discriminating use of different kinds of thinking for different kinds of tasks. This means, for me at least, that cortical—rational—thinking is, and remains, very, very important. It is the kind of thinking used in making the discriminations necessary to use other kinds of thinking; it is the kind of thinking used in writings like the one you're reading; and it is the kind of thinking used in doing the reading.

It's the same in making theatre. I don't want to throw away words, text, dialogue, narrative, character relationships. I want to use them in a fuller range of theatrical expressions. Certainly, the finest works of postmodern theatre show this wish to include, not exclude, to expand the range of thinking, theatrical technique, language—all kinds of languages.

9. Process itself is performance. Rehearsals can be more informative/performative than finished work. The whole structure of finishedness is called into question. If the world is unfinished, by what process are the works of people finished? Why should these works be finished? The world is a reality we are making and changing as we go along. This is the nub of Turner's optimism. The virtual futures we construct are predictions, some of which are being translated into actualities. And this is what a rehearsal does, how it works.

It is not an excuse for sloppiness, lack of discipline, self-indulgence—any of the errors so often associated with process work. It is not a mask for mysticisim or self-serving obscurantism. It is more like the scientific method, through which every assertion is the basis for further investigation, counterassertion, more experimentation, and/or observation, further work.

Kaprow's pieces and Grotowski's series of explorations—Holiday, the "active culture" phase, Theatre of Sources—are examples of process performance. This work is always prey to preciousness, indulgence, exploitation. Nothing stinks worse than rancid sincerity. But still, it is worth the mess. Because process work is the true leading edge of knowledge. Not the historical avant-garde, which is an art movement along with all the rest, but open ways of approaching experience, methods of seeing and dealing with the world.

10. Interculturalism is replacing—ever so tenderly, but not so slowly—internationalism. The nation is the force of modernism; and the cultures—I emphasize the plural—are the force (what word can replace force?) of postmodernism. As a world information order comes into being, human action can be mapped as a relationship among three levels:

PAN-HUMAN, EVEN SUPRA-HUMAN,
COMMUNICATIONS NETWORKS.
information from/to anywhere, anyone

CULTURES, CULTURES OF CHOICE.
ethnic, individualistic, local behaviors
people selecting cultures of choice

people performing various subjunctive actualities

PAN-HUMAN BODY BEHAVIORS/DREAM—
ARCHETYPE NETWORKS
unconscious & ethological basis of
behavior and cultures

This map may scare you. It sometimes scares me. It can be of a totalitarian society, an Orwellian world. But it can also—depending on what people "predict" from it—liberate. It depicts three spheres, or levels, or actualities; but the perforated lines say that a lot of sponging up and down—transfers, transformations, links, leaks—joins these realms, making of them one very complicated system. I mean, without the overarching and the underpinning universals there is little chance for the middle—the multiplicity of cultures—ever achieving harmony, ever combining stability with continuously shifting relations among and in the midst of many different items.

Maybe the most exciting aspect of this map is the possibility for people to have "cultures of choice."

People are born into a culture. They get that culture, maybe some of it before they are even born. Each culture has its distinct ways of doing things; and these ways as much as anything, from the experience of birth on, form individual human beings. Are infants swathed or allowed to run free? Are they nursed on demand or according to a schedule? Are they born into large families, even extended families, where many different people care for them directly, or into small families, even families of one person only, where there is a single caretaker? And so on, through what kinds of food are eaten, who the playmates are, what are the toys, etc. On through all the experiences of living. I don't think this culturing will change. But I do think that very early on—I mean after two or three years—children can be given the experience of different cultures. Again, like second languages, there can be second cultures. And surely, as children grow to an age where they make choices for themselves—and I don't know how my own sense of what this age is is actually determined by my own cultural habits, is not something absolutely fixed—as kids become people capable of making choices, one of the things they must be encouraged to do is to go into several cultures other than the one they were born in. This will be the groundwork for cultures of choice.

Our current view, I think, is soaked with a kind of belief in genetic racism, the assumption that only blacks can be African (in the full black African sense) or that kids from Brooklyn can't be Amerindians. But as cultures more and more come to be performative actions, and information links among them emerge into view, people will choose cultures the way many of us now choose what foods to eat. I'm aware of the cruel irony here: altogether too many of the world's people not only can't choose what foods to eat, but even whether they can eat or not.

"Cultures of choice" may not be "of choice" but a function of the political and economic turmoil of this century: many millions of people have become refugees and/or immigrants. Wars, famines, need for cheap labor, exploitation, adventurism: there are many reasons why people have moved from one culture area to another. These moves, of course, are as old as human history—but I believe they have accelerated greatly over the past 150 years or so. Efficient means of transportation coupled with an ever more integrated world economy, and the particular cruelty and magnitude of this century's wars (not only the wars in/of Europe but wars in Africa, Asia, Latin America, the Middle East: everywhere), have combined to put dozens of millions of people on the road. Many of these people—along with the more fortunate ones, artists especially, who have chosen second cultures (or even third, fourth . . .)—are in a very unusual ontological and social situation. They are no longer part of their cultures of birth nor are they totally part of their cultures of choice. And if they return to their birth cultures—as many artists have done—they find themselves in a situation closely akin to Brecht's *verfremdungeffekt*: distanced even from the familiar. These people are, in a sense, strangers in whatever culture they are in. Or, conversely, they are "almost at home" in more than one culture. In either case, these people are in the position of performers: they are always learning "how to be" in whatever cultural situation they find themselves (by choice or by dint of "crashing circumstances").

There is some actual culture choosing going on right now. Some of it forced on people. In New York City, at the McBurney Y on 23rd Street—about six blocks from where I live—the Thunderbird American Indian Dancers run powwows on a monthly basis. Powwow is itself a form of pan-Indian gathering that developed in the nineteenth century as the Euro-Americans annihilated the Indians and drove them to reservations where they were regarded not as Sioux or Kiowa or Cherokee but as Indian. As it exists in New York—and I think parallels can be found elsewhere—the powwow combines social dancing, ceremonial dancing, socializing, and the display and auctioning of artifacts. Ann Marie Shea and Atay Citron have been studying the McBurney powwow.

> Ironically, despite the possibility that some of the Thunderbirds' ancestors might have inhabited [Manhattan] Island long before any non-native settler, the Y books the powpow under its "international" activities, thus labelling the Native Americans intercultural in their own homeland. This is only one of the paradoxes of the Thunderbird powpows, where Cherokees and Hopis are indistinguishable from Irishmen and Jews, where Santa Claus arrives not to the jingle of sleigh bells but to the beat of an Amerindian drum.[1]

It can get complicated. At one McBurney powwow some enthusiasts showed up for the dancing with top hats and tuxedo elements as part of their dancing costumes. These people had carefully researched what Indians wore to the powwows of the 1880s. The attire that included, eclectically, elements of Western clothing were more authentic historically than the "all natural" feather works worn by many contemporary Indians. But what does authenticity mean? By the 1880s Indians had included in their ceremonial dress many things that weren't originally Indian. People are always doing that. What's different these days—with our ability to preserve on film and in photographs much direct evidence of "how it was"—is also the ability to ransack different periods and select authenticity according to how the evidence is assembled and performed. The enthusiasts at the McBurney powwow were both more and less authentic than the "actual" Indians. My point is that this kind of actuality will increasingly become a matter of choice for all of us—and not simply an unhappy residue of genocide.

To a degree I'm taking up Turner's challenge in this writing. I do not endorse in any sense what people have done to people, or what we as a species are doing to the biosphere. But I do think we have to incorporate our histories, our collective experiences, into our ways of being. That is, because genocide was practiced against the American Indians is no reason to reject the McBurney powwow. Or even to reject its means of culture of choice. That descendants of the ones who committed the genocide are dancing side-by-side with descendants of the victims . . . well, make of it what you will, I refuse to reject this kind of behavior out of hand.

I think that the possibilities for the world are actually very grim. The future proposed by *Global 2000 Report* seems to be what most people are dreaming these days. But, Turner says, if we imagine, and work toward incarnating, embodying, making real what we imagine—and this is close to a working definition of what artists do—then we can bring into existence another future, not the one envisioned by *Global 2000.*

There is a politics of the imagination, as well as a politics of direct action. The politics of direct action is aimed at the injustices of the world. We need that kind of politics. The politics of the imagination is aimed at describing virtual or subjunctive futures, so that these can be steered toward or avoided. The politics of the imagination is real. That is why so much effort is spent by totalitarian regimes, fascist regimes, capitalist industry, and others, to gain thought control and control over human expression. You could almost say these people attempt to control dreaming, the primary process itself. They aim at depriving the people—masses and artists alike—of having imaginative alternatives. Imaginative? Actual alternatives.

For imagination, Turner is saying and I'm agreeing, is an actual alterna-